Inspiring Discipline

A Practical Guide for Today's Classrooms

MERRILL HARMIN

NEA PROFESSIONAL LIBRARY

THE INSPIRED CLASSROOM SERIES

Copyright © 1995
Merrill Harmin

Printing History
First Printing: April 1995

Note: The opinions in this publication do not necessarily represent the policy or position
of the National Education Association. Materials published by the NEA Professional Library
are intended to be discussion documents for educators who are concerned with specialized
interests of the profession.

This book is printed on acid-free paper.   This book is printed with soy ink.

ACID FREE
∞

Library of Congress Cataloging-in-Publication Data
Harmin, Merrill.
    Inspiring discipline: a practical guide for today's schools /by
        Merrill Harmin.
        p.   cm. — (The Inspired classroom series)
    "An NEA professional library publication."
    Includes bibliographical references.
    ISBN 0-8106-2950-X
    1. School discipline—United States. 2. Behavior modification United
States. 3. Classroom management United States. 4. Dignity.
I. —Inspiring Discipline.—II.—Series.
LB3012.2.H37 1994
371.5'0973—dc20   93-30955
                                                              CIP

Contents

Preface

Teachers consistently tell me that today's students are less respectful of authority and harder to discipline. Increasingly, they say that students are responding to threats and punishments with "Who cares?" As one teacher put it, "We can still threaten to keep students after school, reduce their grades, or call their parents. But it's more likely we will get an argument than obedience." Yet there is good news to report. Educators have refined an approach to behavior management that does work with today's young people. And it has practical, everyday strategies that any teacher can use. You will find a collection of these strategies in this book.

As you will see, these strategies take the focus off the negative. They help students build strong expectations that they can and will learn to control themselves. They allow us to stop struggling with students. They give us a way to *inspire* good behavior.

These strategies resemble strategies currently gaining ground in industry. Like schools, industry is finding that rewards for excellent work and consequences for shoddy work are no longer effective motivators. Much more effective are settings where teams set their own rules and procedures, have opportunities to voice personal concerns, and use open discussions to solve production problems and assemblies to rally support for company goals.

The new industry approach is based on mutual respect, not authoritarianism. On collaboration, not isolation. On sharing a vision, not on punishing failure to cooperate. And on the dignity of all, not on praise and rewards for the few.

This book shows teachers the strategies they can use to move in this same direction. These strategies help students feel less that they are being *pushed* to behave cooperatively and more that they are being *inspired* to do so. This idea will become clearer as you read the specific strategies on the following pages. It does not mean, however, that we never push students to control themselves. It does mean that when we do push, we push in a way that is likely to awaken the positive motives in students. We do not push in a way that generates resistance or resentment, or in a way that is demeaning to students. We do not want to solve one problem only to aggravate another. For example, let's say Gene was talking to a neighbor disruptively. We could, of course, threaten Gene with a punishment or embarrass him with a reprimand. That might get him to stop. But it might also make him resent us or even want to retaliate someday. Or it could cause him to withdraw from future learning, at least until the smart of our reaction diminishes. A threat or reprimand might even reinforce any feelings Gene might carry that he is not a worthwhile person and, perhaps, can never become one. Furthermore it is not particularly pleasant for us to spend our teaching days issuing threats or embarrassing students.

Fortunately, strategies exist that allow us to handle disruptive side talk without such negative side effects. For example, an alternative strategy, one you will find in this book, would have us simply say, without negative emotions, "I need you to be quiet now, Gene." Another strategy would have us redirect Gene's attention: "Gene, would you read the next item to me?"

Even if Gene did not stop his bothersome behavior,

there are steps we can take that are neither punitive nor embarrassing. This collection, for example, includes a strategy for talking to Gene about the problem that is likely to increase his cooperation, not reduce it. You can expect to find many strategies for handling such behavior problems. If one does not work or feel right to you, others might do the trick.

Those of us who teach must control misbehavior. But some ways of doing so are better than others. In assembling this collection I have sought ways that seem least likely to cause future problems and, whenever possible, most likely to teach students valuable lessons about self-control and dignified social living as well.

These strategies work for many reasons:

- *They address the need for dignity.* The strategies help teachers to teach with dignity and students to learn with dignity. They help us treat even the seriously disruptive student with full dignity. The strategies gradually strengthen self-discipline and self-respect.

- *They bring out our best.* The orientation of the strategies in this book brings out the best in students. It makes it easier for students to apply themselves to schoolwork. It also brings out our best qualities, our creativity and confidence, for example. We can then more easily handle all our teaching tasks, including the challenge of the seriously disruptive student.

- *They enhance living/learning integration.* This book's approach serves us now and serves students later. It helps reduce confrontations and negativity. As a result, we enjoy teaching more, and students learn healthful ways of dealing with personal and social problems.

- *Problems become nonevents.* This book's approach drains heat from disciplinary incidents. It gets us to reframe what we once saw as very disturbing events—a student refusing to work, for example—into ordinary parts of the teaching job. These strategies help us approach such incidents as we approach lesson planning, grading, and other teaching chores, not so much as personal confrontations but as inevitable, ordinary parts of the job. Consequently, disciplinary problems are not nearly so upsetting.

- *They activate the power of expectations.* These strategies also help us expand our influence beyond what we do. We know of course that physicians who prescribe with strong intentions and positive expectations produce superior healing. For teachers, too, strong intentions and positive expectations make a difference. The strategies in this book help us utilize this power.

- *They serve the big picture.* Consider three general tasks of teachers: (1) to run classes smoothly and efficiently each day, (2) to get students learning subject matter, and (3) to handle the first two tasks in ways that serve society. Our basic charge, of course, in that third task: to help students become productive,

HOW TO USE THIS BOOK

This book is divided into two parts. Part I contains an assortment of strategies that help a teacher build a cooperative classroom climate, a climate that reduces the likelihood of problems arising in the first place. The strategies of Part I also help dissolve the antagonisms and resentments students bring to class from elsewhere in their lives. These strategies get students more ready and willing for classwork. Part II contains the strategies for more directly managing student behavior. Some are geared to elementary students, some to high school students, and some to all students.

ZIGGING AND ZAGGING

It is not necessary to read these strategies in the order they are presented in the book. When I lead discipline workshops I find it useful to zig-zag between the prevention strategies of Part I and the problem-handling strategies of Part II. My pattern is to start with a few strategies from Part I, so that teachers might see how they can get more positive energy into their classrooms. Not all teachers need this, but many teachers draw new ideas from those strategies.

I then introduce some of the basic behavior-management strategies from Part II. As teachers are adapting those strategies to their own situations, we consider additional climate-strengthening strategies. Then we look at other management strategies. You might follow such a sequence yourself.

GETTING A BUDDY

However you proceed, I recommend that you do not go it alone. These strategies almost always work better when you have one or two colleagues with whom to share ideas, reactions, and experiences. One person is apt to interpret a strategy this way, another that way. One person is apt to create this new spin-off, another that variation.

In general, I recommend that you go through the strategies and pick and choose the ones you think might work for you. Give them a test. With a buddy or two, talk over what you found, what questions come up, what suggestions you have that might help others. Proceed in your own way, following your own time clock, whatever is best for you.

YOUR PERSONAL DISCIPLINE PLAN

I also recommend creating your own plan for preventing and handling the behavior problems that exist in your situation. Use the ideas in this book and any others you know or can create. Prepare yourself to do more than improvise. When it comes to discipline in the classroom, I do not recommend winging it. That often leads to inconsistencies and backtracking, which complicate matters substantially.

Whether you are experienced or just beginning, I recommend writing out a comprehensive plan of action: What strategies do you want to use to prevent problems in your classroom? What do you want to use when problems come up, as they likely will, no matter how well you teach?

Some teachers make a chart of what to try first and second and third, and so on. Create enough of a discipline plan so that you feel ready to tackle whatever comes up. We do almost everything best and easiest when we feel most secure.

WHERE THESE STRATEGIES COME FROM

These strategies come from all of us, from the accumulated wisdom of the profession. I know I did not create them. They come from many years of reading the research and hearing what teachers say works. Some of those reporters are listed in the bibliography, but I could not begin to list all the many who contributed.

One person deserves special mention, however, Grace H. Pilon, the creator of *The Workshop Way*®. I remember a public school in New Orleans, Danneel School, in which Pilon was a consultant. Danneel is a large K-8 school in a classic urban slum. In one year I saw that school transformed from chaos, with clamor and fighting and destruction aplenty, to a place of relaxed routine. After one year, students not only exuded good will, but, when arguments broke out on the playground, the students often settled the problems that arose peacefully by themselves.

More impressive than the transformation itself was the means by which it was managed. Neither fancy equipment nor superteachers were added to that school. Nor was an extensive in-service program added. The teachers in the school, not a few of whom seemed close to burn-out, were simply given a special set of instructional and class-management strategies. They worked. Pilon's strategies were not only very effective but also straightforward enough that almost *any* teacher willing to give them a go could improve teaching effectiveness substantially.

You will find in this book ten strategies directly adapted from that work. They are identified in the glossary. Consider observing for yourself some of the teachers around the country using Pilon's design. To identify such teachers or to obtain publications that detail the many strategies Pilon developed, contact Workshop Way, P. O. Box 850170, New Orleans, LA, 70185-0170 (Telephone 504-486-4871).

GOING BEYOND THIS BOOK

When you truly get the sense of this approach of inspiring discipline, you do not really need this array of strategies. You can use your own methods and inventions, flowing fully in the creative art of teaching. You might want to use this book at the outset, for illustrations of what inspiring discipline might look like, or to sharpen or confirm your own understandings, and then move out on your own.

How can you be sure you grasp the distinction between inspiring discipline and non-inspiring discipline?

You have it when you know, for certain, that if you ever had to expel a student, you could do so with everyone's dignity intact, both yours and the student's. You will not say with bitterness, "This will teach you a lesson." The student will not be hearing, "I hope I never see you again." Rather you can imagine yourself apologizing, "I wish I knew how to help you behave better right now. I'm truly sorry I don't." You can imagine the student knowing someplace inside himself or herself that it is hard for you to expel anyone, that you would truly like to do better by him or her, but that now you simply do not know how.

You have it surely when you live your own life with growing dignity and remain aware of the potential in others to grow in dignity. And don't forget teaching. Teachers of course need more than effective discipline strategies. They need to know how to keep students actively involved in learning. You do not want bored students or idle time, time students can use to make mischief. You want to maintain active involvement in a way that builds classroom cooperation. It is not always easy to get that result with the restless, disrespectful students we increasingly find in schools. But it can be done. For practical suggestions, see the companion volume to this discipline book, *Strategies to Inspire Active Learning* (Harmin, 1995). It contains tested strategies that get students to listen carefully in lectures, participate responsibly in discussions, attack homework with diligence, expand their time on task, and do anything else you need to keep students actively, productively involved—in a way that is *inspiring* to students, that keeps drawing forth the students' best qualities.

For those instruction strategies and for other publications detailing the practices and theories of the inspiring teaching approach, or for information about on-site demonstration and training programs, contact Merrill Harmin, Inspiring Strategy Institute, 105 Lautner Road, Edwardsville, IL 62025 (Telephone 618-692-0177; Fax 618-656-5663).

PART I

Establishing a Climate of Cooperation

CHAPTER 1

Building Community in the Classroom

"GETTING ALONG" AS A CLASS OBJECTIVE

The purpose of this strategy is to inspire students to think about what they can do to improve the way they live and work together and to keep students moving toward that objective. The strategy entails the teacher announcing that "getting along and working well together" will be a class objective. The teacher then takes actions to keep that objective in sight over the long term. This strategy can be applied whenever the teacher finds it appropriate.

One way teachers can help students become a genuine community of learners is to set "getting along and working well together" as a class goal, and work with students to achieve that goal.

For instance, Ms. Tse might announce to her class: "From now on I would like us to aim to become a class that practices good living as well as good learning. I want us to get along together, help one another, be supportive of each other. I want us to work together as a healthy, happy, cooperative community of learners. I want us all to enjoy being here in class each day."

Such an announcement might be made the first day of school, or it could be made after a class has gotten underway, to signal the start of a new era. "So far we've focused on learning," a teacher might say. "From now on, I want us also to be aware of *how* we learn. I want us to focus on being a class that not only learns a lot, but learns in ways that are good for us. I want each of us to feel that being here makes us stronger, more open, more creative, and more confident. I don't want learning to go on in ways that make anyone feel weaker, or less willing to work with others, or less confident."

An announcement of this kind is especially meaningful to students who do not expect a teacher to be concerned with anything more than the amount of material they have to learn. It opens students to a new expectation, and the power of that expectation can make a difference. When students expect that the group will work in ways that are good for everyone, students will help bring that about.

Once the objective is announced, the teacher can use the expectations it creates in many ways. Some examples:

• I hear grumbling about the assignment. Grumbling does not seem to me to fit a group that is working happily, positively. I wonder how we can do better?

• This group is really working well together. I especially like the way we are helping one another, keeping our procedures working smoothly, and going out of our way to reach out to those who might feel left out. Thank you for all that. I appreciate it very much.

The following strategy, *truth signs,* helps enormously in working toward the creation of a community of learners in the classroom.

TRUTH SIGNS

The purpose of the truth signs strategy is to teach a class key truths about what constitutes an effective, healthy learning community and to provide guidelines to help them become such a group. The strategy involves explaining key truths about effective learning, such as "It's OK to make mistakes; that's the way we learn." The teacher also posts these key truths on signboards to serve as constantly visible guidelines. This strategy is most effective when used early in a course.

The signs used as part of the truth signs strategy are not the usual ones seen in classrooms. They do not tell students what to do: "Think before you act." "Respect the rights of others." "Raise hands before speaking." Nor do they threaten. These signs remind students of important truths for learning and living.

Introducing Truth Signs

The following lesson illustrates how one teacher introduces truth signs to a class.

First, the teacher points to a sign posted on the wall, or holds the sign up for students to see. The teacher reads it aloud: *"Everyone needs time to think and learn."*

"Now," the teacher says, "let's read this together: 'Everyone needs time to think and learn.' Let's say it again, with power." The class repeats, with more intensity.

"It's true," the teacher says. "When we hear something or try something, we don't usually learn it right away. It takes a little time for us to make sense of it, get it inside us. Even if I say something simple, like, 'My mother was born in England,' it might take a second for you to make sense of what those words mean.

"I want to post this sign on our wall so we remember it. It's an important truth. And it can help us keep our learning climate healthy. You can use it to remind yourself to give yourself enough time when you want to learn something. You don't want to rush it. Why?

Because, as the sign says, everyone needs time to think and learn.

"Let's read the words aloud again, together, to help us get it more fully inside ourselves. All together: 'Everyone needs time to think and learn.' Again please, with more power."

Second, the teacher says, "Let's look at another sign: *'We each learn in our own ways, by our own time clocks.'* Let's say it all together. And again, this time with more power.

"We each learn in our own way, no one quite like the other. Some learn best from words, some from pictures, some from experimenting, some from talking things out with other people.

"And we each learn according to our own time clocks, some fast, some slow, but only when the time is right.

"For example, I didn't learn to spell very well until I was older. My time to learn to spell just didn't come when it came for most others. But when the time was right, I became a fairly good speller. You might have had a similar experience. How many of you tried to learn something, or were told you *should* learn something, but it just didn't work until you were older, until somehow the time became right?

"Yes, it is true that we each learn in our own ways and by our own time clocks. We want to remember this sign. Let's say it again together, this time with energy.

"We'll keep this sign in our classroom along with the first one, to remind us of this truth. Sometimes we forget it. We may think we *should* learn something the way others are learning it. But their way may not be the best for us. We have to search for our own best way to learn.

"Or we may think we should have learned something *already*, because others have already learned it. That may just get us down on ourselves, and that will make it harder for us to keep our energy up and keep on learning.

So please don't get down on yourself if you don't learn the way other people learn, and if you don't learn when other people learn. That would be foolish, for we each learn in our *own* way, by our *own* time clocks, right?"

Third, the teacher shows the students another sign: *"It's OK to make mistakes. That's the way we learn."*

The teacher says, "Let's say that all together. And again.

"Even the first time we walk, we stumble around, fall down, get up, try again. The first time we try anything new we are apt to make a mistake, until we get it.

"It makes no sense to get down on ourselves when we make a mistake. We can eventually get so afraid of making mistakes that we're afraid even to try—and that's silly. The truth is that it's OK to make mistakes. That's the way we learn. That's just what happens when we start learning.

"All together again. Once more, saying it like you mean it! We want to remember that mistakes are not unfortunate. They are necessary. They're the way we learn."

Fourth, the next sign reads: "It's intelligent to ask for help. No one need do it all alone."

"I don't have to be able to build cars and grow food and construct roads and design clothes," the teacher says. "I just need to know how to do what *I* do. No one has to know it all.

"If I need to do something I can't do, it's intelligent to ask for help from someone who can do it. Then I get what I need and, often, the other person gets the pleasure of helping. Doesn't it make you feel good sometimes when you help someone? That's what a community of people does. They help one another. One person delivers the mail. Another mows the lawn. One cooks. Another builds. Old folks sit outside and smile on us. Young people play outside and act silly. It takes all of us to make a community. No one has to do it all alone. We can help one another.

"In fact, it's *intelligent* to help one another. It would be a mistake for someone to try to do everything alone. So, please, in this class, if you need help, if you don't know what to do, or if you need someone to explain something, ask for help. It's intelligent to ask for help. Everything works better that way. We can become one happy team, one community, that way.

"So, all together now. Let's say it again, with lots of power!"

Fifth, the teacher asks the class to look at one last sign: *"We can do more and learn more when we're willing to risk."*

"Let's say you want to try something new, or talk to someone, or speak up in class," the teacher says. "What you want to do might *seem* like a good thing to do, but it can *feel* risky. That often happens to people. We want to do something. Our minds say it would be good to do it. But our feelings say hold it, it's risky! Looking ahead, we feel it's risky to act.

"What then? Should we stop? Sometimes the risk is really too great. We might get hurt or hurt someone else. Then it would be smart to stop, not to do what we thought of doing. But sometimes the risk is really not that large. There is no real danger. It just *feels* risky.

"What we can do then is call on our courage and go right through the anxiety. Speak out, if that's what we wanted. Or join a new group. Or whatever it is we wanted to do. The key is a willingness to act, even when it feels risky, even when acting will feel uncomfortable. Then all we need to do is call up our courage and get started.

"When we can call up our courage that way, we can do more and learn more. When we can't, we often do nothing. We are stuck in inaction. We may not even be able to think straight about the situation. We may become limited to doing only what feels very comfortable.

"But when we are willing to make use of our courage, we can think about whether or not there is real danger and, if not, we can get going and do it, even though we know starting will be uncomfortable.

That is why we can do more and learn more when we are willing to risk.

"Sometimes it helps to have support from others. It's often easier to take a risk when we're not alone. Can anyone here think of a time when having someone to support you made it easier to act?

"By the way, did you know that all people have courage? Courage is a natural ability of people, like speaking and dreaming. Some people can call up courage easily. Some don't have much practice at doing that. Famous people, even actors, sometimes get anxious in public. But they are usually good at calling up their courage and getting out in public anyhow. Have any of you ever felt it would be risky to do something and then called up your courage and did it anyhow?

"It's easier to risk when we can call up the courage inside us, and it's easier too, as I said, when we don't have to go it alone. One other hint: It is also easier to risk if we are willing to accept *not* succeeding.

"Sometimes it seems so important that we win, or come out on top, or get everything turning out just right. It becomes so important that we get nervous before we begin. A part of us doesn't even want to begin. We forget the simple fact that things don't always turn out the way we like. But if we can accept that fact, if we can remember that people sometimes win and sometimes lose, we won't worry so much about losing. If we lose, we can try again another time. It's usually not the worst thing in the world. And then taking the risk becomes easier.

"How many of you sometimes are very afraid of not winning? Do any of you back off and stop trying in such situations? How many would agree that when people can accept winning or losing, however things turn out, they'll be less nervous and, if they are not so nervous, might even be more likely to win?

"If there is something good for you to do in this class, I hope you will be willing to do it. Even if it feels a bit risky.

"Let's repeat the sign together! And again, saying it like you mean it!"

The teacher closes by saying, "We'll keep these signs posted as reminders for us and we'll talk about them again from time to time. But now let's look back at all five.

"Which ones do you feel good about? Which do you think might help you learn in this class?" The teacher points to one sign. "How many feel good about this one? How about this sign?" The teacher voices an approximate count for each sign, to acknowledge the students who raise their hands.

"Finally," the teacher says, "write me something that you got out of this lesson. You might write endings to one or more of our outcome sentences." The teacher points to the list: "I learned...." "I was surprised...." "I'm beginning to wonder...." "I rediscovered...." "I'm feeling...." "I promise...."

Some General Suggestions

Truth signs is one of the strategies I have adopted from Grace H. Pilon's 1988 work. It is one that teachers report works well at all grade levels. I myself use truth signs in university courses at the graduate level.

Each teacher, of course, should use his or her own style in introducing truth signs, and in choosing which signs to introduce. In my university classes, I usually present and post all five included in the preceding lesson.

In regard to the risk sign ("We can do more and learn more when we're willing to risk."), it is prudent to distinguish between a smart risk and a foolish risk. I might tell students that I see a smart risk as one that would have positive outcomes. A foolish risk might have dangerous or hurtful outcomes or in some way not be good for oneself or for others. It would be foolish, I remind students, to call up courage and do something that should not be done in the first place. Some teachers have asked students to create a chart of smart and foolish risks and they report that students enjoy doing so.

I have used a discussion on risks to lead into a discussion of smoking, drinking, or sex. "Can you think of a time," I might ask, "when it takes more courage to say no rather than yes?" I might then have students role-play situations, to solidify the relationship between risk taking and intelligent choosing in ways that have meaning for them.

I recommend against using more than six or seven signs in one classroom. I would not want to dilute the power of those signs. Other truth signs, however, may be appropriate. Some suggestions:

We each must live our own lives. No one can do it for us.

It's not possible to know the full potential of another person.

Life is one step at a time, one day at a time.

If it happened, it happened. Let's go on.

We can accept and support one another. No one need be all alone.

The hardest part of any job can be finishing it.

We can allow ourselves to be our whole, true selves.

There is no best in the world of people.

Such signs communicate important truths about learning and living. It is easy for any of us to forget these truths. It is often heartening, reassuring, and invigorating to be reminded of them. *Cushioning,* a strategy described below, provides a meaningful way to continue such reminders throughout the year.

A mother wrote:

I have a son, age seven, second grade, and a daughter, just turned five, preschool. Often at dinner we share information about our days, in particular "what we learned in school." I have discussed the "truth signs" you taught us with the children and have tried to incorporate them into everyday living. One day last week my children were in the kitchen and I was in another room. I heard my son become exasperated with himself over something he had not done correctly. I then heard my daughter say, "Jed, it's OK to make mistakes. That is how we learn." Out of the mouths of babes…

CUSHIONING

The purpose of cushioning is to minimize fears related to learning and to produce confident, active learners. The strategy entails the teacher reinforcing truths about learning with questions ("Is it OK if someone gives a wrong answer today? Why?") and reminders ("As you tackle the homework, remember that you do not have to understand it all tonight."). Cushioning is most effective if used frequently, and especially before students are asked to participate.

Just because a teacher posts a sign saying it's OK to make mistakes, there is no guarantee that students will not feel anxious about participating fully in class.

Signs are most effective when they are treated as only a first step in a process of reducing learning anxieties and creating confidence. A steady offering of reminders and support is almost always necessary. Pilon (1988) calls her strategy for doing this *cushioning*.

The following dialogue is an example of cushioning. The intent is to "cushion" the anxieties students might feel during the lesson, so that they can relax, learn with confidence, and learn fully.

> **Mr. Montoya:** Class, before I ask my questions today, I would like you to guess why I don't care if you make a mistake. Can you guess why that wouldn't bother me at all?

Michael: Because you want to know how much we know. Mistakes show what we don't know.

Mr. Montoya: Yes, you could say that. Anyone else?

Jackie: As the sign up there says, it's OK to make mistakes, that's the way we learn.

Mr. Montoya: Yes, that's true. Anyone else?

Tomas: It shows we're trying, risking it, even if we don't know for sure that we're right. And we learn more when we're willing to risk.

Mr. Montoya: Yes, all that is true. Our signs remind us of those truths. Now let's get to the questions....

Besides the immediate goal of helping students relax, there is a long-term objective for using cushioning: to help students achieve a genuine understanding of the truth about mistakes—that they are a natural part of the learning process, that they are certainly OK, and that they can reduce students' fear of making mistakes by reminding them of that truth and, in that way, students learn an important life-management skill.

Note that, in the above example, Mr. Montoya used cushioning *before* the lesson. Imagine if he had waited until after a student had made a mistake and then asked the class if it was OK to make mistakes. The class might have said yes, but the student who made the error probably would have been embarrassed at being the apparent cause of such a discussion. Besides, if Mr. Montoya had not begun with that discussion, the lesson might have proceeded with students needlessly anxious about making mistakes.

The next day Mr. Montoya says, "Before we begin this lesson, I want to remind you that no one need learn this material perfectly today. Why do you think I say that?"

Alex: Because it's new material.

Mr. Montoya: Well, it is new. But I would say that even about old material. Why is it OK if someone has not learned something perfectly on any day?

Christa: Because we all learn in our own ways, by our own time clocks. It might not be time for us to get something.

Mr. Montoya: Is that true, class? (The class agrees and the teacher continues.) Fine, so go as far as you can. It won't help you to feel bad if you fail to get it all today. Now to our lesson....

It's day three, and Mr. Montoya has just asked a question. Rob raises his hand. Mr. Montoya says, "Rob, before you give your answer, let me ask you, 'is it okay with you if I say that your answer is not the correct one?' "

Rob: I guess so. But I wouldn't like it!

Mr. Montoya: I can understand that. But is it *OK* if you make a mistake, even if you don't like it?

Rob: Sure.

Mr. Montoya: Can anyone tell us why it would be fine if Rob's answer turns out not to be the correct answer?

Rob: (Piping up before anyone else can answer) Because it's OK to make mistakes. As the sign says, that's the way we learn.

Mr. Montoya: Thanks, Rob. Now let me repeat the question and hear your answer.

On day four, Mr. Montoya says, "Class, before we begin, let me ask, 'is it OK for some of you to fully understand this material and some to still be totally confused?' "

Christa: Sure. We all need time to think and learn. Some of us didn't have as much time as we need.

Mr. Montoya: Thank you, Christa. Anyone else?

Luís: Some of us might not be interested in this so much.

Mr. Montoya: Thank you, Luís. Anyone else?

Barry: We all learn in our own ways, by our own time clocks.

Mr. Montoya: Yes, and how does that truth free us from feeling bad if we don't get this material at all? How does it make it OK for some of us to know it and some not to know it?

Gilbert: Maybe it wasn't our time to learn it yet. (No one has another comment.)

Mr. Montoya: Thank you, class. It's also possible that you didn't yet have your own *way* of learning it. So don't feel overly proud of yourself if you've gotten this already, but on the other hand there's no need to feel bad if you haven't gotten it yet. A lot has to deal with whether or not your time and way for learning have shown up. Anyhow, let's go at today's work with an accepting, open mind, helping each other as best we can.

Mr. Montoya begins day five by saying, "Today I'd like to start off by asking why you think it's smart to ask a friend for help if you are confused. Anyone?"

Nita: We can't all ask you all the time.

Denise: Sometimes it makes me feel good when someone asks me for help.

Mr. Montoya: Yes, thank you. Anyone else?

Kurt: I'd say because we all learn more when we help one another.

Mr. Montoya: Fine. Just remember that sign. Let's read it all together again.

Class: We can accept and support one another. No one need be all alone.

Mr. Montoya: Now for today's lesson....

The Three-Step Cushioning Process

Repeat the following three-step process often, perhaps every day. Students who need reassurance will appreciate it. Others seem not to tire of it.

1. *Creating awareness of a truth.* Although a teacher could start by simply stating a truth such as, "It's OK to make mistakes as we get into this lesson," students usually get more involved when the teacher starts with a question, for instance, "Will it be OK if people make mistakes today?"

2. *Inviting thought.* The teacher then invites a brief dialogue, to refresh understanding and deepen feelings of assurance and confidence. Student comments are accepted.

3. *Making a concluding comment.* The teacher makes a concluding comment and moves promptly into the lesson. Cushioning is not meant to take more than a minute.

Variety helps keep the process alive. Here are some additional opening statements teachers can use:

• Do you have to know everything today? Why not?

• Does anyone here have to be perfect? Why would I not expect that?

• I'd say it's OK if someone forgot what we learned last week. Why might I say that?

• Some of us expect too much of ourselves. How many are sometimes like that in a classroom? Do any of our truth signs help us with that?

• It might be unfortunate, but is it OK for someone to have forgotten to bring a notebook today? Why?

- What if someone knows a lot and others know a little? I'd say that's not important. Maybe it is not the *time* for the others to know it. Besides, the others can practice asking those who know for help. That's good for everyone. Which signs talk about some of that?

- I'd say knowing the right answer is not as important as being willing to risk thinking and offering an answer. Can you guess why I'd say that?

- What is the best way to handle a failure? What would be the smart way to react?

- It takes courage to be willing to risk when you aren't sure of the outcome. How many would agree? Disagree?

- No one can ever be me, and I cannot be anyone else. What does that say about how we can best learn here?

- My worth as a person does not depend on how much I know. Why do you think I say that?

- More than right answers, I need courage to hunt for answers. How about you?

- Sometimes it takes courage to say, "I don't know." But sometimes that is the honest answer to a question. Can you say why it sometimes takes courage to be honest that way?

Some additional suggested concluding comments:

- No one knows everything. No one ever will. So just relax and get what you can from this.

- Each of us is intelligent; it's just that each of us is intelligent about different things. You will find your own intelligence as you go through life.

- No one in life has to know everything. We each help each other. Our job is to live together as a helpful community.

- All people are unaware of some things. We are just unaware of different things.

- All human beings make mistakes. So, what will you make if you're human? Mistakes!

- It's not mistakes that are important, it's what we do after we make a mistake.

- Failing at a task is not as bad as many people seem to think. Can you imagine what would happen if people were always afraid of failing? So let's just put it behind us and get into today's lesson.

- I'd like you to relax and use your full awareness here. Be a confident learner. No need to worry here. So risk jumping in wholeheartedly, thinking only of what you are doing. Trust that the outcome will be OK.

The Essence of the Cushioning Process

The great strength of cushioning is that it reminds students that it is all right to be oneself. Cushioning provides a practical way to help people digest that truth and, thereby, to accept themselves—blemishes, tempers, and all. This is often a very liberating kind of learning. It is a good example of the truth setting people free—in this case free to get into lessons wholeheartedly.

MASTERY OF STUDENT PROCEDURES

The purpose of the mastery of student procedures strategy is to prevent misbehavior and confusion about classroom procedures. The strategy involves the teacher spending enough time teaching classroom procedures so that students can easily follow them.

It is easy to assume that students will understand and follow simple procedures: "Pick a partner and talk over last night's homework." "When you replace your folder on the shelf, replace it in alphabetical order." But some students will neither understand nor smoothly follow such directions.

The remedy is to overteach procedures, especially at the beginning of a course and with elementary school students. Aim for all students to feel absolute mastery of procedures and to feel good about that mastery. For young students, it's often wise to walk through a procedure, giving explicit instructions:

> When I say, "Get a partner," first look around and make eye contact with someone. You can sit with someone nearby or not, as you choose. But if I ask you to pick someone you haven't worked with recently, you might have to stand and walk elsewhere to make that eye contact. Then sit near that person, as close as you can comfortably, so that your talk can be quiet. Let's try that. Pick a partner you haven't worked with recently, and sit with that person. Please go do that now.
>
> (After students begin to get settled) Let's talk about this. Chances are some of you felt anxious about being left out, that it was risky to get partners. As I look around I see that some of you were in fact left out. It was tempting to make a trio instead of a pair, or to sit by yourself, or to come and ask me what to do. Please go back to your original seats and let's try this again.
>
> This time, when I say "go," take a risk and don't rush to sit with the first person you see. If most people are paired up and you're still without a partner, look to

see if anyone else is left alone. A person might not have felt up to taking a risk today, so you may find someone sitting quietly alone. That sometimes happens. Take your time and look closely, like a detective looking for someone. If you have done that and still find no one without a partner, please make one trio. Ask a pair if you might join them. Let's try it again. Please get yourself a partner with whom you haven't worked recently. Go.

Similarly, the instruction to a group "Talk over last night's homework" invites confusion, which invites noncompliance, which invites discipline problems. To head off such problems, one teacher posts a chart that reads: "HOMEWORK GROUPS: Compare answers. Talk through disagreements. Help each other understand. Check with another group if unsure. Support each other in mastering the content."

Another teacher has a different chart for writing assignments for which there are no specific right or wrong answers: "FOR WRITING HOMEWORK: 1. Exchange papers. 2. Read thoughtfully. 3. Make helpful feedback notes. 4. If there is time, talk over your reactions."

Spend enough time to make procedures perfectly clear and acceptable to all. Get students to enjoy their ability to follow guidelines masterfully and smoothly. The increase in student efficiency will more than compensate for the investment of teacher time.

INTELLIGENCE CALL-UP

The purpose of the intelligence call-up strategy is to remind students of their intelligence and inspire them to think through problems by themselves. The strategy calls for the teacher to make a continual effort to generate students' awareness of their native intelligence, including their ability to stop and think and make wise, responsible choices. The strategy should be used frequently throughout the year.

Pilon (1988) stresses the value of repeatedly telling students they are smart enough to solve problems on their own. Employing the intelligence call-up strategy, this is how one first-grade teacher announced that thoughtful problem solving would be the style in her classroom:

> When things are not flowing smoothly in this class, I want you to pause and ask yourself, "What would be the smart, intelligent thing to do?"
>
> So, for example, if papers are not being piled neatly, or a crowd is forming at the door, I might say, "What would be the smart, thoughtful way to handle this? Think about this and then go ahead and do what you think would be best."
>
> Let's use our brains. We want this to be a class in which we all learn how to think for ourselves. Let's grow our intelligence. I'll remind you of this from time to time.
>
> If you were not a human with a human brain, you might not know what is best to do. But you have an amazing brain. You can think for yourself. You do it all the time at home.
>
> When things are not going right, pause and ask yourself, "What is the smart thing to do now?" Learn to reason things out for yourself. Humans can do that like no other animal.
>
> Can anyone give an example of when something was not going smoothly, and you stopped and thought about what was best to do, maybe what you had to do or stop doing, and you did that?

Some incidents from an eighth-grade class illustrate how the intelligence call-up strategy can be used.

In the first instance, students failed to clean up on time. The teacher said, "Class, we're having difficulty getting everything cleaned up on time. How can we handle this problem? Let's brainstorm a list of ideas on the board. We are smart enough to find a way to solve this that will be good for us all. After the brainstorm, we'll see what we think is best."

In another instance, several students were shunned by classmates when the teacher asked them to get into pairs. The teacher said, "Class, I'm having to use extra time to pair up everyone when I call for sharing pairs. I can understand that you want to sit with your good friends. But this is taking us too much time. Besides, I want us to learn to get along with everyone here. From now on, please reach out to all students, even those not near you. Be generous and kind. You will know when it is a good idea to do that. Be aware please. Make sure everyone gets a partner quickly."

In another instance, preparing a class for the arrival of new students, the teacher said, "Here's a chance to exercise our brain power. We will get new students from time to time. What would be the best way to get them into the flow of our work? We could talk it over now and use our creativity all together. Or would it be better to ask a committee to think it through and give us a recommendation or two? What do you think is best?

When a student asked a question about a nonvital issue, the teacher said, "You decide," in a tone that conveyed, "I trust you to exercise your awareness and self-management abilities wisely."

When two students came to the teacher complaining about each other, the teacher said, "Talk it over. If necessary, write down what options you have, and work it out yourselves. Use your creative intelligence. You both decide."

The intelligence call-up strategy often has teachers asking students, "What would be the smart thing to do? Stop and think and you'll know what is best." The teacher using this strategy keeps talking that way, trusting that all students will eventually know that he or she really means it. Eventually all students will come to believe it, and the intelligent way of handling situations will become second nature to them. Hold high expectations and enlist the power of those expectations.

Assuring Students They Are Intelligent

Some students of course do not believe they are intelligent. Perhaps their parents confuse grades with intelligence, or compare one child to another. Perhaps earlier class experiences did not fit the students' learning styles. Any of these factors may have led students to discount their ability to think and live intelligently.

The best way of assuring students of their intelligence may be simply to keep using the intelligence call-up strategy so that students actually experience themselves being intelligent. But you may want to find a way to talk about intelligence to students, especially to help them distinguish human brain power from school grades.

I like to do this by telling about my father, who never got to high school, never did much reading, but who was one of the smartest people I ever knew. He knew what was going on and he knew what would likely happen next. I talk about him and then ask:

> What does it mean to be intelligent? It's certainly not a matter of being able to remember facts or solve school problems. Some of you can do that better than others. But *all* humans can do much more.
>
> All humans are aware. And all humans can manage that awareness. Look at that window. Now look at the ceiling. That is managing your awareness. You're directing your attention where you want it. All humans can do that. When you think about what to do next, you're simply managing your awareness, focusing your awareness on the options ahead. Being intelligent is nothing more than that, directing your awareness where you want it. The better you can manage awareness, and the more things you can bring into awareness, the more powerful your intelligence will be.
>
> In this class I encourage you to practice that intelligence. Reach to become more aware of what is going on around you and inside you, including inside your head where, if you're patient enough, you'll find lots

of good ideas. And including the world around you where, if you listen and observe closely, you'll notice many interesting events.

And reach to become better at managing that awareness, focusing it for longer periods of time on one thing, looking more closely at details and looking more widely at the general scene. Practice that and you'll learn how to use more of your native intelligence.

In class, when you're unsure of what is best to do, pause and become more aware of what is going on. Then reach for all the ideas you can dream up. Perhaps ask others for ideas too. As our sign says, "It's intelligent to ask for help." After you get ideas about what can be done, imagine what will happen if this is done or that is done. That's what it means to think ahead. Think like that and your natural smartness will get exercised. It'll help you to live an intelligent life. Like my father did.

CHAPTER 2

Dissolving Antagonism and Resentment

CLASS AGREEMENTS

The purpose of the class agreements strategy is to communicate teacher respect for students' thoughts and feelings. A related purpose is to provide a means of nurturing a cooperative class climate. The strategy calls for the teacher to outline plans for the class and invite student agreement. The teacher can also invite students' suggestions. The class agreements strategy can be used whenever it seems appropriate, as frequently as every day or perhaps only when the class is starting a new unit.

Few of us react positively to bossy people. When people push at us, our instinct is to push back or to step aside. However, when people reach out to us, when they invite us to join in an activity, we are likely at least to consider cooperating. One approach teachers might use to enlist student cooperation is *lesson agreements*. A teacher could, for example, ask for agreement on a day's lesson outline:

Today I planned to start with our homework. Then I thought we would begin our discussion on France. After that, there would be time for your group-project work. And if time remains we could do some map work. How does that sound? Can we agree on that plan?

Some students might have suggestions. Some of these might justify a change of plans. It would be up to the teacher, however, to make that determination. The idea is not to get all to agree. It is, rather, to use a moment or two to demonstrate respect for students, invite collaboration, and hear suggestions, so that the teacher can move ahead with maximum cooperation.

Another approach is *course agreement*. This invites acceptance not of one lesson but of a long-term plan. For example:

> Rather than touch on all the topics in the book, I would like us to handle a few topics with depth and care. Here are the topics I recommend.... Any reactions to that suggestion? Can we agree at least to start off in this way?

Course agreement should not be perceived as an invitation to anarchy or idleness. The teacher should remain firmly in control. This approach is simply an invitation to new and better ideas and a spirit of responsible cooperation.

Lesson agreements and course agreements start with a teacher's plan. In some cases it is appropriate and wise to use a *cooperative planning* approach to involve students in the development of the plan. When the teacher and students agree, the resulting plan typically generates high levels of student commitment and motivation. For example:

> How shall we handle this next unit? Let's brainstorm and make a list of some options. Then let's see if we can agree on how best to proceed.

COMMUNITY LIVING LESSONS

The purpose of community living lessons is to increase appreciation of what is involved in living as a cooperative classroom community. The strategy calls for the teacher to offer examples that define healthful community living and to inspire students to become such a community. The strategy should be revisited periodically, especially when it appears that students could be doing better at living and working well together.

Fewer discipline problems erupt when groups see themselves as cooperative communities. Teachers will do well, then, to use strategies that get students working as a team, accepting one another, respecting one another and the teacher. One way of doing this is to refer to one of the signs introduced as part of the truth signs strategy. "It's intelligent to ask for help. No one need do it all alone. That's part of living happily together," the teacher might say. Remind students what a functional neighborhood looks like: One person drives a bus. Another paints a house. A third walks home carrying groceries. Each person does something different, yet all do these things as part of the community.

Another way to strengthen the students' sense of community is to post two new signs:

> We can aim to be a group that is all for one and one for all.
> We can accept and support one another. We need not ignore or reject anyone.

Consider pointing out the connections between the class as a community and two American principles: *democratic government* and *individual freedom.*

Democratic government means that authority resides in the people. This kind of government has the following characteristics:

- collective decision making
- government of the people, by the people, for the people

- no arbitrary laws or cruel punishments
- laws based on open-minded discussion
- a balance of powers to limit misuse of power
- each citizen sharing in group responsibilities
- respect for the common good
- one nation with liberty and justice for all

Individual freedom means, among other things, the following things:

- freedom to speak one's mind
- freedom from unnecessary duties and controls
- the right to life, liberty, and the pursuit of happiness
- equal opportunity
- respect for individual differences
- the Declaration of Independence
- the Bill of Rights
- searching for better ways
- free enterprise

Teachers advance the principles of democratic government and individual freedom by striving to live them in the classroom. Through this modeling, teachers help students prepare for mature citizenship. Teachers' reminders to students of the principles of democratic government and individual freedom can be concluded with this challenge: "Let's learn how we can live and learn well together here, each with the right to manage his or her own work, each with the responsibility to avoid interfering with others' rights, and each with the opportunity and responsibility to play a respected part in the group as a whole."

To communicate what a healthful community means, one teacher had students wear name tags the first week so they could get to know one another more quickly. He also talked about teamwork in sports and in factories. He said he wanted his class to learn to work together as a "great team." That particular class decided to give itself a class name, to exchange phone numbers so students could call each other if they needed help with homework, to set up a hospitality committee to welcome new class members, and to have occasional class outings on weekends.

Another teacher began the school year with the phrase, "One for all and all for one," challenging her class to be stouthearted enough to keeping working for that class spirit, even when it was hard to do. Later she used two quotes (from Brendtro et al., 1990) to initiate discussion of what a community classroom might be:

> The circle is a sacred symbol of life... Individual parts within the circle connect with every other. What happens to one, or what one part does, affects all within the circle.
>
> —Driving Hawk Sneve

> He drew a circle to shut me out.
> Heretic, rebel, a thing to flout.
> But love and I had the wit to win.
> We drew a circle that took him in.
>
> —Edwin Markham, *Outwitted*

By using images of a smoothly functioning family, a friendly neighborhood, or an effective team, or teaching the basic principles of society, teachers can inspire students to work toward becoming a mutually supportive and respectful community of learners. Because this is not a familiar goal for many students, teachers must remind them from time to time of the community ideal.

How to Handle Classroom Rules

Although no teacher wants to generate misbehavior, a teacher's priority should not be to control everything students do so that behavior problems never come up. Some problems can be valuable for teaching students what is involved in living and working as a classroom community. Accepting this will affect how a teacher views classroom rules.

The intelligence call-up strategy (see chapter 1) reduces the need for a set of rules. Rather than relying on rules, teachers remind students that they are intelligent beings, smart enough to make informed, appropriate choices, just as they do every day at home and on the street. A teacher using this strategy would tell students something like this: "Think through the situation you face. What are all your options? What would be the smart thing to do? When you use your brain power, you'll see what makes the most sense. Let's live together here as one supportive, intelligent community."

The intent is to teach students how to handle problems, as they will need to handle them as mature members of their community. Some teachers, however, still feel the need for specific rules or, more precisely, behavior guidelines. Consider these two approaches to establishing guidelines:

> **Teacher A:** We will need certain rules of behavior in our class if we are to work effectively. Perhaps rules about speaking out or disturbing others or getting work in on time. What rules do you think we will need here? Let's discuss this and brainstorm a list. (Later) Now which rules on our list are most important? How shall we handle those who violate rules? What would be appropriate consequences for such violations? How will we remember these rules and their consequences?

> **Teacher B:** I want us to get along well together. I want us to live and learn together much like a healthy community or family, with respectful give-and-take. I want us to help one another when that is appropriate, and leave others alone when we judge that that is the wise thing to do. Some guidelines might help us become such a community. One guideline might be, "Honestly yet respectfully, let someone know when he or she is bothering you." One I personally need is, "Do not leave the room without a hall pass." What other guidelines might we consider? (Later) How can we keep to those guidelines and avoid slipping off them? How should we react when people make mistakes, as all humans do?

Both teachers might end up with behavior guidelines: Raise hands before speaking, no hitting or running, and so on. But the second teacher is likely to elicit more goodness and cooperation from students. And because nurturing goodness and cooperation is a concern of teachers, we can use our discipline plan to further our purposes. A discipline plan, then, need not be an unfortunate necessity. It can be a valuable tool both to prevent problems and to promote personal maturity.

Even in classes that can use rules, I recommend announcing early on, talking much like Teacher B, that we expect the class to learn to live together as a productive, learning community, as a classroom in which everyone gets along well together, respects one another, lends a hand when needed, and leaves people alone when that seems to be the better choice. That, of course, is the overarching purpose of the strategies articulated in this book.

HAND-RAISING SIGNAL

The purpose of the hand-raising signal is to provide a means of making a quick, effective switch from small-group discussions to teacher talk. The strategy calls for the teacher to raise one hand. Students who see the raised hand then raise one of their own hands, and all students then see that it is time to stop talking. The strategy is appropriate to use when the teacher wants students to discontinue discussions among themselves.

Disorder invites misbehavior, especially when students work in small groups. The hand-raising signal is a strategy that helps keep group work orderly. Imagine a teacher explaining to a class:

> When I raise my hand during small-group time, it is the signal to stop your group discussions. Whenever you see my hand go up, please raise your own hand. Then people facing away from me, who cannot see me, will see hands go up and they can raise their hands. If you are talking when hands go up, please finish your sentence, but do not start a new sentence.

If something important is interrupted, which will sometimes happen, please remember what it was. I may simply need to give you new directions or ask you to speak more quietly. Even if there is no more time for you to continue your group discussions, if you remember what you wanted to say, you can say it to others later, perhaps during lunch or after school.

THE "ONCE" PRINCIPLE

The purpose of the "once" principle is to free the teacher from the need to repeat directions. This strategy also provides a means of teaching students to listen responsibly and catch up appropriately. When using this strategy, the teacher announces that from now on he or she will give directions only once; students who miss the directions are to find an intelligent way to catch up. This strategy is best used as early in a course or school year as possible.

Imagine a teacher saying:

Please, everyone, look at me. From now on I will say things only once. Page numbers. Directions. Anything like that. So please practice keeping yourself aware. If you miss what I say, find a way to catch up. Perhaps whisper to a friend or watch and see what others are doing or later catch what you missed. Call on your intelligence. You'll know the best thing to do. Now to today's lesson....

Note that the teacher said that only once. He or she did not say, "Any questions?" That might have led to a repetition of the message. Note also that the teacher began by asking all students to look at him or her. If a direction is to be given only once, it is fair to call for attention so that all students have a chance to hear. Confusion is prevented by giving directions only after a call for attention and a moment of silence.

Once students realize that when they ask the teacher, "When was that due?" or "What did you say the page was?" and the teacher only smiles and says nothing, not even "I told you" or "I say things only once" or "Please check with a neighbor," students manage just fine. If a teacher communicates an expectation to students that they will manage the "once" principle, they will. Indeed, experience shows that it is more difficult for the teacher to stick to the "once" principle than it is for students to learn how to live with it.

THE WHOLE-SELF LESSON

The purpose of the whole-self lesson is to help students learn to accept themselves, accept others, and be open to becoming the best that they can currently be. The strategy calls for the teacher to explain that all humans have both "narrow" and "open" selves. The teacher also explains that when the narrow self shows up, as it does for everyone, it is wise to be accepting, for acceptance opens people to their open selves and thus allows them to be their "whole selves." This strategy can be used whenever it seems appropriate.

The whole-self lesson helps students *and* teachers become more accepting of themselves, even when they are not being their best selves. What follows is an example of the whole-self lesson. It is in a form I have used when working with a group of teachers. Consider each step in that lesson as if you were in the teacher group. That will probably best prepare you to craft a version of the lesson for your own students.

A Whole-Self Lesson with Adults

First, let me talk a bit about myself. I am a person who, as I see it, experiences several selves. For example, I am sometimes my easy-going, open-minded, flexible self. That is a self I have inside me these days, for these are fairly good days in my house and, if the winds are just right, I can be that self. I call that my *open self.*

At other times I am much more self-centered, narrow-minded, irritable, tight. I don't feel at all easy and flexible. I call that my *narrow self.* Alas, I can also be that way nowadays.

Figure 2-1

Four Selves

A former self	My current narrow self	My current open self	A possible future self
Lonely	Self-centered	Easy-going	Peaceful
Withdrawn	Narrow-minded	Open-minded	Loving
Passive	Resistant	Relaxed	Content with whatever comes up in daily life
Unconfident	Picky	Generous	
Suspicious	Insensitive	Flexible	
	Abrupt	Humorous	
	Irritable	Accepting	
	Confused		

Check the list I've made. (See Figure 2-1.) I've put four of my selves on it and a few qualities that describe each. I first noted one of my former selves. That's a self that showed up for me when I was much younger and rarely shows up nowadays. I suspect it lies dormant inside me. I hope it stays dormant.

Then I noted my current narrow and open selves. Finally I added what feels like a *possible self,* a self that is not now available to me but that I sense exists deep inside me someplace, a self that might emerge as an available self. I occasionally get a hint that it's a possible self for me.

Try drawing up a list for yourself—or, I should say, for your *selves.* You can skip the inclusion of your former and possible selves if you like. It's most important that you write notes describing your current narrow and open selves. See what turns up for you.

Most of us feel more comfortable when we are our open selves than when we are our narrow selves. Should we regret it when our narrow selves show up? Is that unfortunate? Wouldn't it be far better for us to learn how to live always as our open selves?

Try it if you like. But you may find it is not possible.

A toothaches comes. A disappointment occurs. We look in a mirror. It rains at the wrong time. Lots of things happen that get us feeling off balance, tight, uncomfortable, not at all our open, balanced self. As I see it, humans naturally experience both narrow and open selves. It is part of the human condition. Events show up that throw us. No way of escaping it. Does that make sense in your experience?

Furthermore, I don't believe we can expect to have one open self for an entire life. Rarely is a child's open self the same as his or her adult open self. Even as an adult, if I were my current open self for a long time (and that has never happened), chances are I would not be satisfied until I became something different, something larger, something in the direction of my possible self. Soon enough, my open self would no longer feel so complete to me. Perhaps that is what maturity is all about. It seems to me related to the idea of becoming the best we can be, or developing our full potential.

I don't believe humans are meant to live only in their open selves. We have both narrow and open selves and humans naturally spend time in each. It makes no sense, then, for me to try to live only as my open self. I have to remind myself of that from time to time because I have a tendency to get down on myself when I am my tight, narrow self and not my easy-going, open self.

I also don't believe humans outgrow their current selfhood and move to a new selfhood before the time is right for that growth. A child cannot be an adult before the time for that arrives. An acorn cannot become an oak at any old time. It makes no sense, then, for me to regret that I have not yet become my possible self, the self I sense I might someday be. I have to remind myself of that sometimes when I realize that I am not as far along as I sense I might be.

As you might imagine, I sometimes need to say to myself: The sun does not rise before sunrise. Things are what they are. Me too. I am not yet better than I now am. Furthermore, I am not always as good as I sometimes am. Sometimes I get into my tight, narrow self. No sense getting down on myself for that.

How are you at accepting yourself when you remain in your current stage of selfhood? If you do not accept yourself, you might notice that you are being your narrow self. So the most general question is: How well do you accept yourself when you are being your narrow self?

I would like our classrooms to make it as easy as possible for students to accept themselves, even when they are not being their best selves. The reason is simple: When we are not accepting of ourselves, we have two problems, rather than one.

The first problem is not being as good as we might be, that is, not being fully ready to use all the best we have in us. Imagine yourself being your narrow self. Can you see that you would not likely be expressing what is best for you and those around you? So, that's our first problem: being in a state in which the best in us is not easily available.

If we accept ourselves, we can work on that one problem. Let's say I am angry, so angry I can't think straight. If that is my only problem, I can say that this too will pass, ups and downs come, and I might even be able to do something to make it pass more quickly. Say something positive to myself. Walk among the trees. Think of my wife's lovely ways. Whatever.

But if we do *not* accept ourselves, we have a second problem. So I, for example, might not only feel anger, but also feel guilt, frustration, or self-blame, feeling I should not be angry. I don't want to be angry. I want not to be what I am. That makes it harder to keep going. Certainly harder to think clearly about what's going on and what I might do next. Indeed, being down on ourselves for being down is often the larger problem.

In truth, when we do not accept ourselves when a narrow self shows up, as sooner or later it will, we are rejecting a part of ourselves and that, if it becomes habitual, leads to all kinds of ills, mental and physical. It is not empowering to reject oneself.

I recommend we practice accepting ourselves as fallible human beings. We make mistakes. Moods change. For one reason or another, from time to time we find ourselves in our uncomfortable, narrow selves. That's just the way life works.

When I have slipped, and when I notice it, I like to say, "Well, there I go again. I'm being my narrow self. But no sense getting down on myself for that. Time to move on!" Sometimes I find it useful to say that aloud, sometimes to the people around me. Such an admission makes it easier for me to avoid feeling even more down.

How about you? What works to help you accept yourself when you notice that you're your narrow self? If you have trouble, remember Mark Twain's explanation of why you are less than perfect. "Man," he said, "was made at the end of the week's work, when God was tired."

Let me now talk about my *whole self*. No mystery here; it is all of me. If I were to return to the line above where I listed my selves and put a circle around what are now my narrow and open selves, the circle would represent my current whole self. For good or ill, that's me. Want to know yourself better? Simply return to your own list of selves and put a circle around it all.

When sages tell us, "Know thyself," I believe they want us to know the parts in our circles. When sages tell us, "Accept yourself," I think they want us to accept our whole selves. And when my own father told me, "Be yourself; don't put on airs," I think he was giving me the same message. What do you think?

Give these ideas a test. See if they serve you in some way. Here are two experiments I recommend.

First, try calling up your open self some time when you believe it would be especially useful to you. You might wait for an important appointment. Or you might wait for the next time a tricky choice comes up. Perhaps you'll want to do several things and not be sure what to do first. Or perhaps you'll not want to do something and yet feel pressure to do it. Or perhaps there will be *nothing* you want to do and you're unsure what to do about *that*. Or perhaps some pattern or habit of yours you dislike will show up and you'll wonder how to handle it.

When such an occasion arises, pause and say to yourself, "How would my open self handle this situation? Or, what would my open self want me to do?" You may have to ask yourself the question several times until you get the hang of it. If you repeat the activity, log the results of each event and see if you can learn something from the trend.

Or try calling up your whole self the next time you feel off, tight, anxious. And then say to yourself, "Now wait a minute. I am now being my narrow self. I can see that. But that is not *all* of me. I sometimes will be other than the way I am now. Let me not forget that."

See what happens. Again, you might find it useful to log the results. I should add that if you never again feel your tight, anxious, or narrow self, you'll have no need to worry about this second experiment.

Bringing the Whole-Self Lesson to Students

Here's how a third-grade teacher presented the whole-self lesson to her class. It may provide ideas that you can adapt for use with your students.

1. I told the class about my own open and narrow selves. (I didn't talk about my former self or my possible self. I wasn't sure their concept of time could handle that.) I made two circles on the board, filled in several qualities of my open and narrow selves in each, and then asked students to fill in two circles for themselves. (Whole class: five minutes. Individual writing: two minutes.)

2. I asked for three volunteers to read any one quality of their open or narrow selves. Almost everyone volunteered so I called on five students. Then I asked all of them to sit in pairs and either share some of their notes or talk about what I had said about myself. I didn't want to force talk if students wanted to keep things private. They all seemed to go at this with energy. (Whole class: two minutes. Sharing pairs: five minutes.)

3. I then talked about it being OK when we are our narrow selves, how it happens to me (they laughed) and how it happens to everyone. I asked if some would describe what happens when *they* become their narrow selves. They talked about tests and scolding. This produced lots of comments that everyone could identify with and lots of good-natured smiles all around. They all seemed to recognize their common humanity. (Whole class: five minutes.)

4. Next I asked them what helped them become their open selves when they felt "off" and we made a list on the board: playing with friends, hugs from mom, and so on. These students seemed to have a much better perspective on life than many of us adults. I believe this step opened up new ideas to some students. (Whole class, list created: four minutes.)

5. Then I told the class I wanted to explain more about this. I said I would talk and, when I paused, I wanted them to think and make notes. I gave three mini-lectures on the whole self. I started by drawing one large circle around my two circles and labeled that my whole self. Then I talked about how I and people we studied in history have whole selves, and how each student has a whole self. I ended by recommending that they appreciate their whole selves, especially when they feel like failures or when someone treats them badly. "We all have narrow-self times," I said. "But as humans," I said, "we also have open-self times. We are whole human beings." (Whole class: speaking and writing, five minutes.)

6. After they made their last notes, I had them think about all we had talked about so far. I asked them to write some of their learnings from the lesson by completing such sentences as: "I learned...." "I rediscovered...." "I'm beginning to wonder...." "I was surprised...." After a minute or two, I asked if anyone would read aloud something he or she had written. Almost all the hands went up, so I whipped

around the whole class and offered each student a chance either to read a sentence or to say, "I pass." No one passed! (Individual writing: two minutes. Whip around: about ten minutes.)

Summary notes: The lesson led to lots of new ideas for the students. Several said they better understood their parents and why parents sometimes seem upset. Two said they wanted to take the lesson home, to see what others thought were their narrow and open selves. I had several students refer to their "bad selves." I just suggested they call it their "narrow" selves and they seemed to do that afterward. Later that day, I heard one boy say to another, "I was my open self on the playground, wasn't I?" They seemed to get it. I'll follow up in some way, although I haven't decided how yet. I think I'll invite all students to ask their open selves for advice next time they have a choice to make.

Some Follow-Up Possibilities

Once the whole-self concept has become familiar to the class, it is natural for students to talk about their open, narrow, and whole selves. These words become powerful tools in the effort to increase appreciation of oneself and others, and of the magnificence of life in general. One teacher put up a new sign to keep the whole-self lesson alive: "We can accept our narrow selves, call up our open selves, and in that way be our whole selves."

Speaking of the whole-self lesson, one college teacher said, "It's a running, lighthearted gag now. Since I taught that lesson, when I or a student is 'off,' someone is apt to suggest that the person is stuck in narrow selfhood. Almost always when that suggestion is voiced, everyone, including me, the person who most often is 'off,' relaxes, even smiles. Not bad at all."

One high school physical education teacher said, "I know they learned it because I hear things like this: 'I'm my open self today so I should do well,' and, 'Be your whole self, man, don't get down on yourself.' "

A sixth-grade teacher reported: "Students now use being in narrow selfhood as an excuse, as 'I can't do good work today because I'm my narrow self'.... It's not that they didn't give excuses before. But although they talk more about narrow selves, they *act* more like open selves, so I am happy to say something is working."

THE "BE" CHOICE

The purpose of the "be" choice strategy is to teach students how to bring out their own best qualities, and to help teachers bring into the classroom the personal qualities they most want to express. The strategy calls for the teacher to show students how to choose the way they want to be (e.g., persistent, courageous, accepting). Teachers themselves use "be" choices (e.g., to be confident that students will cooperate). This strategy can be used whenever the teacher considers it appropriate.

Some teachers, from day one, have very few discipline problems. Students naturally offer them respect and cooperation. Some of these teachers keep a tight rein on their classes, and some are easy-going, so the absence of discipline problems is not a matter of strictness or leniency.

What does make the difference? It is the extent to which teachers are perceived by students as caring and confident, as opposed to defensive and vulnerable. The teachers who students sense are in touch with their strengths, ready to handle whatever comes up, and sincerely interested in the well-being of their students are the ones who maintain the most constructive tone in their classrooms.

Teachers who cannot readily communicate care and confidence can learn to do so, but not simply by wishing it were so. Teachers can learn, little by little, in part by getting their nonprofessional lives working well, whatever that might entail, and in part by practicing the "be" choice strategy.

What Is a "Be" Choice?

"Be" choices are different from "do" choices. Note how often we must choose what to do: Should I phone my friend? Should I go shopping? Should I do this now or later or not at all? Some days we make a detailed to-do list. These are "do" choices. We choose what we *do*.

Less often we make "be" choices. Yet we can make "be" choices as often as "do" choices. If I go shopping, for example, there are several ways I can be. I can be efficient, aiming to get in and out of the store quickly. I can be friendly, taking time to smile at open faces. I can be adventurous, on the lookout for new foods to try, new corners to explore, new people to meet. There are many ways I can be when I go shopping. And I can choose which of these ways to be: efficient, friendly, adventurous, thrifty, or whatever. I can even choose to be without a "be" choice, spontaneous, open to whatever happens. All of these are "be" choices.

"Be" choices sometimes make all the difference in the world. Let's say, for example, that I choose to phone a friend. And let's say this friend is a tricky person for me to talk to. It might be well for me to pause and consider how I want to be during the call. Do I want to be my accepting, listening self? My assertive, straight-talking self? My open-minded, flexible self? There are several ways I can be when speaking to this friend. If I deliberately choose a way to be, it is much more likely that I will, in fact, be that way, which might make a difference in the outcome of the conversation.

When people use the "be" choice strategy, then, they pause and choose how they want to be in the time ahead. I usually use it when I make my lesson plans. At the top right corner, I write how I want to be as I teach that lesson. Often I'll write, "Be flexible, tuned into students." Other notes I often write are "Be clear and brief" and "Be energetic and upbeat." It depends on what I sense the students most need for that lesson. I also like to teach the "be" choice to students.

Teaching the "Be" Choice

When I teach students the "be" choice, I start by distinguishing between "do" and "be" choices, in much the same manner as that explained earlier in this section. I make the distinction by offering examples of my own "do" and "be" choices. Then I might say:

> Let's try making a "be" choice here. In a moment, I will ask you to look around the room for, perhaps, ten seconds. As you look around, please be your ordinary self, just as you might look around the room if I were busy and you had nothing else to do. No talking, just looking around. Start now.
>
> Thank you. Now let's do that again, but this time I want you to write a "be" choice before you look. Let me give two suggestions. Perhaps choose to be your curious self. Be on the lookout for something new or interesting. Most of us have curiosity inside us so, if you like, you can look around as your curious self.
>
> Or perhaps choose to be your careful self, looking closely at details, not letting your eyes slide past something too quickly, really looking at whatever your eyes see.
>
> So choose now which way you would like to be, curious, or careful, or some other way, and write your personal "be" choice on a piece of scrap paper. Writing a "be" choice makes it more certain inside ourselves. (Pause.) OK, please look around now in the way you wrote you would be.

After asking students to share any differences between their two looks around, I might then say:

> Please write on your scrap paper how you want to be for the rest of the lesson today. You can't always choose what you will do, here or anyplace. But you can always choose how you want to be. Right now in class, for example, you might choose to be relaxed, or intelligent, or careful, or happy. What are some other ways a person could be in a class like this? (I then listen to them describe their ideas.)

Choose any way you want to be and write it down now. Writing it usually plants it more solidly in your awareness. If we have time, I'll ask you later if that "be" choice made any difference for you today.

I might follow that experiment with the following remarks:

In general, I recommend you experiment with "be" choices. After school, for example, you might pause and ask yourself how you want to be when you walk in the door at home. Or if you see some friends ahead, pause and choose how you want to be as you meet your friends. Want to be your cooperative self? Your leadership self? Your energetic self? Experiment with whatever seems interesting to you. Perhaps next time I'll ask if someone would be willing to share his or her experiences.

I also like to talk about "be" choices when a conflict arises, a real one or a conflict the class is studying. For example:

The labor-management conflict we read about ended with no real winners. How could it have been handled differently? Notice how both parties took a win-lose position. Both were being confrontational. What would have happened, do you think, if one or both sides paused and made a different "be" choice? If, instead of being confrontational, they chose to be open, seeking a resolution both might agree on so that if they found a solution there would be no losers?

Another example:

I would like to sit with you two and talk about the fight you had yesterday. As I understand it, each of you thought that you were right and the other was wrong. And both of you were being stubborn, insistent, conflictful. Let's imagine that one or both of you paused before things got too bad and made a different "be" choice. Let's say you chose not to be stubborn but, say, open about the argument. You chose to be open-minded and to try to see the whole picture. And let's say you asked someone to sit with you two, to help you talk about the argument and better understand the whole picture. Can you see how that might have prevented some of the worst of what happened yesterday? Can you see how someone in a conflict could, in fact, pause and choose not to be conflictful, but to be open-minded? Tomorrow, I'd like to role-play such a situation. You two can play yourselves in the skit or we can get others to play the parts and you can watch. We'll talk more about this kind of "be" choice tomorrow.

Although the "be" choice helps many students in several aspects of schooling and living, it is included here because of its special power to balance students in their less conflictful, more open selves. When making a "be" choice, students rarely choose to be irritable, impatient, or angry. Given a choice, they almost always choose aspects of their more open, peaceful, productive selves.

If I had already taught the whole-self lesson to my students, I might incorporate the following into my remarks:

You can choose to be your open self if you like. Of course, you may not remain your open self even if you choose it, for you also have a narrow self. But if you *choose* to be your open self, chances are you will more often or more fully be that way than if you made no choice at all. Experiment and see.

The "Be" Choice to Reduce Misbehavior

The "be" choice is my best strategy for marshaling my confidence and projecting my care for students. When I make a lesson plan I often write "Be confident and caring" in the top corner of my plan.

No matter what I write, even if I write, "Be open-minded and flexible," or "Be spontaneous and lively," I find I teach with relatively high levels of care and confidence because I sense that the "be" choice helps me display my best self. It helps me teach as someone who knows himself. Indeed, when I make a "be" choice, I am someone who *chose* his self.

In any case, I know that the "be" choice helps me project a positive personal power and I strongly suspect that teachers who project positive personal power have fewer discipline problems. You might want to play with this strategy. See if you can use it to help you bring out the selfhood you want to make evident to your students.

The Open-Self Choice for Handling Misbehavior

If the "be" choice helps prevent problems, it also helps teachers handle problems when they do arise. For a moment, imagine a mother scolding a boy who has just messed up the kitchen, and not for the first time. This mother has lost it:

> How many times do I have to tell you? You are impossible! This is the hundredth time you messed up like this. Get out of here! I'll tell you one thing: You'll be sorry you did this!

There are lots of *"you"* statements in that outburst. What is the likely outcome? A withdrawn, vulnerable boy might experience hurt and an urge to pull away. An outgoing, assertive boy might find urges to resist welling up in him.

By contrast, picture the mother doling out a scolding while somehow remaining in touch with her larger, open self. This mother has not entirely lost it. Her outburst has lots of *"I"* statements:

> I can't take this anymore! I want you to know how impossible this is for me! I need some order, neatness in the kitchen. Even more, I need respect for my property! I don't know what to do anymore! All I can tell you now is that we must do something about this situation!

This scolding will likely communicate less bitterness, less blame. Rather, it communicates a mother unable to tolerate messy kitchens any longer, suffering an overflow of frustration.

What is the likely outcome of that second scolding? A withdrawn, vulnerable boy might identify with the mother's plight and feel an urge to be kind. If he were more outward and assertive, it would not be surprising for him to apologize and offer to help clean up. (For more on *"I"* statements, see the *honest "I" statement* strategy in chapter 3.)

The moral of the story: How we are being makes a difference. Be your whole self, the self that has access to your good, wise, strong, open qualities, and you will likely handle problems with more personal balance, in ways that are most likely to produce positive outcomes, and least likely to generate negative side effects such as resistance, defensiveness, rebellion, and retaliation.

Put another way, a teacher's style—strict or lenient, loud or quiet, passionately expressive or thoughtfully reserved—is less important than what *motivates* his or her behavior. The healthiest motives are those that flow when a teacher stands as an open self, open to the best wisdom, passion, and care inside himself or herself. The "be" choice can be used to help one make the transition to that self, which is the self most likely to elicit student cooperation and respect.

Essentially, it's not only what we do that counts; it's also how we approach what we do. Which approach produces the best payoff? An approach, I would say, that enables teachers to be their best selves. A sign mentioned earlier in this chapter addresses this: "We can accept our narrow selves, call up our open selves, and in that way be our whole selves."

PART II

Managing Student Behavior

CHAPTER 3

Recognizing–and Respecting–People's Limits

THE SIMPLE AUTHORITY STATEMENT

The purpose of the simple authority statement is for teachers to exercise authority with minimum distress and emotion. By employing this strategy, the teacher can also show students how a person can use authority respectfully and reasonably. The strategy calls for the teacher to voice disapproval authoritatively, promptly, and as unemotionally as possible. The strategy can be used when misbehavior requires teacher intervention.

Teachers have both the authority and the responsibility to keep student behavior within bounds. Sometimes that requires teachers to disapprove of what students are doing. The trick is to convey disapproval in ways that sustain respect for both the teacher and the student.

As teachers, we need to accept our responsibility and communicate our authority easily, comfortably, firmly, but never harshly:

• When you say, "No, you may not leave now," you do not want the student to hear, "You should know better than to ask," or, "What a silly question," or, "Don't bother me with such questions."

You do not want the student to feel stupid, or slighted, or put down. You want the student to hear the statement simply as a fact, the responsible adult's position.

• When you say, "That's just too much for me," You do not want to sound apologetic or weak. And you do not want the student to think you're saying, "You should not want to act the way you are acting."

You simply mean that you have limits, that you, too, are a human being. Too much talk or rattling or whatever is going on is in fact too much for you. Furthermore, you want the student to hear, "I know you are willing to make that reasonable adjustment for me, for that's what people do when they live together in community."

• When you say, "We do not do that here," you do not want the students to feel chastised, just informed. You do not want resentment, just clarity.

You do not want them to think you're really saying,"You should have known better than that." You want the student to hear your statement as, "You did not understand this, so I'm giving you the information."

• When you say, "No, that's not correct. The answer is Washington," you do not want the student to think, "Too bad. I was hoping I was right."

You want the student to think, "Oh, I see. Washington is the answer. I'll remember that for the future."

• When you put a finger to your lips to signal someone to shush, you do not want the student to feel guilty or bad or irresponsible.

You want the student simply to think, "Oops, I should stop talking. The teacher is reminding me of what I already know myself."

• When you say, "Sit down this very minute. Take control of those impulses," you do not want the student to feel you are being hostile and punitive or that the student is a defective or uncontrollable person.

You want the student simply to notice that you are taking charge at a time when his or her self-control has temporarily failed and that you are doing what is necessary to protect the welfare of all. You want the student to feel that you are on the side of safety and learning, not against anyone.

The simple authority statement is similar to what Ginott (1972) calls a "sane authority message." Ginott says it would be "insane" for a teacher to belittle a student who has lost self-control or to suggest a student should not be feeling what he or she is in fact feeling.

Figure 3-1
"Insane" and "Sane" Deliveries of the Same Message

Insane	Sane
You two stop talking. You have no consideration for those who are working.	This is a quiet time. We need it to be absolutely silent.
You have no right to be angry. You know the rules. You must wait your turn.	I know you are upset. The rules sometimes work out that way. But now I really need you to wait your turn.

Guidelines

■ **NO HOSTILITY** Generally I recommend that statements of disapproval be emotionally neutral, like a red traffic light. A red light does not communicate criticism or malice. It does not blame or sting. It just gives a signal to stop.

Authority statements should be similarly straight and simple, similarly unemotional and noncritical.

Sometimes a teacher can use a playful touch when exerting authority. For instance, when a student is fussing in a way that is too distracting, I might simply pause for a split second and glance his way with a wink or smile.

Sometimes a joke is effective: "Let me finish this please. I've been waiting all vacation to give this speech."

A simple but effective tactic is to keep talking and walk by the student, or touch the student gently on the shoulder. Not a sting, but a touch of care.

■ **NO HESITANCY** Authority statements should be made promptly and cleanly, not hesitantly or apologetically. Students should see the teacher as strong enough to speak forthrightly, with no need to apologize for his or her responsibilities. But students should see themselves as strong too. Each should sense, "The teacher clearly sees me as strong and smart enough to take straight talk."

■ **WITH AUTHORITY COMES DISCRETION** My own tendency is to voice disapproval more often than is necessary. I like a smooth-running classroom and am often too quick to respond to bumps in the proceedings. A boy may be walking aimlessly about the classroom. Very likely something in me would jump up ready to disapprove. Yet saying nothing might be the better choice. The boy might soon enough get back to work. Or he may not be disturbing others more than they can easily handle. Even if it is not easy for the other students, it might be better to remain quiet. The students might need to call up their powers of concentration, or their power to resolve conflicts among peers. There is some advantage to giving students the opportunity to stretch in those ways.

When a teacher rushes to solve problems that grow out of healthy community living in the classroom, it sends a signal that he or she does not trust students to handle those events on their own. That assumption sets up expectations that the teacher will handle all group behavior problems and probably slows the development of students' responsibilities for healthy community living. For all those reasons, teachers should be sensitive to the possibility that they might sometimes intervene unnecessarily.

■ **BODY LANGUAGE** Body language can also be used to make a simple authority statement. Here is an example adapted from an idea by Fredric Jones in Charles (1992, p. 84):

1. Sam and Jim are talking while the teacher explains fractions to the class. The teacher makes eye contact, pauses momentarily, and then continues with the explanation. If Sam and Jim continue to talk...

2. The teacher pauses again, makes eye contact, and shakes his head slightly but emphatically. He may give a fleeting palm-out signal. If Sam and Jim continue talking...

3. The teacher calmly walks over and stands near Sam and Jim while explaining, and increases student involvement by saying, "Now everyone work this problem on your scratch papers." If Sam and Jim still keep talking to each other...

4. The teacher makes eye contact with each and calmly says, "Jim, Sam, I need you to stop talking right now."

■ **BRIEF EXPLANATION** Many teachers consider it wise to include a brief explanation with a disapproval. For example:

• Please do not touch that material now, Dennis. I'll need it later for my demonstration.

• I want no one here ever teasing anyone in this school. I'm the kind of a teacher who gets very upset when I hear others being put down in any way.

A brief explanation highlights the reasonableness of authority statements. That makes them sound less arbitrary, easier to accept. Long explanations, however, should be avoided. They suggest that a teacher does not trust students to understand, or does not expect them to accept the teacher's authority. A lack of respect for students' intelligence or common sense often underlies a teacher's need to provide long explanations.

Explanations are most effective when they are maximally truthful and personal. Compare these two statements:

> **Teacher A:** Everyone must have work in by Wednesday at 3 p.m. I cannot get my evaluations in on time if any work comes in after that.
>
> **Teacher B:** Everyone must have work in by Wednesday at 3 p.m. It is difficult for me to handle the papers and budget my time if work comes in after that.

Teacher B's authority, I would say, is apt to be easier to accept. Students are more inclined to believe that it is "difficult" to handle the paperwork than that it "cannot" be done.

Another instance in which Teacher B's words are likely to be heard as being more truthful and personal:

> **Teacher A:** No running in the halls. It's a school safety rule, and I must enforce it. People who run in halls get hurt. So watch yourself and never run in any hallway.
>
> **Teacher B:** No running in the halls. It's a school rule. More important to me, I don't want to see you or anyone else get hurt. Running in halls too often produces serious injury. If you see others running, please ask them to walk fast and avoid hurting themselves or someone else.

■ **WHY EXPLAIN?** Explanations are especially valuable when the motive of the teacher is not clear to students. The teacher's motive, as I see it, is at the heart of effective classroom limits.

Some teachers who are very strict are fully respected by students, often very much appreciated by them. Similarly, some teachers who are very lenient are fully respected and very much appreciated by students.

However, some teachers who are very strict are not respected at all. They might even be highly resented. Some teachers who are very lenient are not respected at all. What then is important?

I believe that space and boundaries are important. I believe it is important that students are not constrained by too small a space—that they have enough space to express at least some of their talents and initiatives. I also believe that it is important that boundaries are not so wide as to be invisible to students. Boundaries can provide both safety and guidance. In short, I believe the central issue is the extent to which students perceive boundaries as being for the good of all, for the students and the teacher, not being imposed by the teacher in any self-serving or uncaring way.

Explanations can often clear up student misunderstandings about boundaries. If students see the limits as too tight, explanations can make it clear: "I the teacher really need those limits now so I can best teach you," or "You need these limits now even though you may not fully appreciate it." The message is: "I am doing the best I can to care for you." Similarly, if students need more guidance or security, explanations can communicate, for example: "I the teacher do not feel comfortable in being more controlling than this right now" or "You may feel insecure, but you need to learn to manage your own life, and this freedom can help you to do it." The message again is: "I am doing the best I can to care for you."

Our motives, then, are critical. As long as we are not too controlling or too lenient, students tend to accept, even appreciate, authority, if students know that our motive is to do what is best for them.

REDIRECT STUDENT ENERGY

The purpose of redirecting student energy is to end misbehavior without creating negative feelings. Instead of focusing on the misbehavior, this strategy calls on the teacher to turn student attention to something else, preferably something worth attending to. It is useful when direct confrontation is either unnecessary or imprudent.

Martin keeps tapping his pencil, making a loud noise. A simple authority statement might call for the teacher to walk over to Martin while talking to the class and touch the arm holding the pencil or, if that did not stop the noise, take the pencil from him, perhaps with a smile, commenting, "Take your pencil from my desk later, when you feel more settled."

The strategy of redirecting student energy might call for a teacher to get Martin more involved in the lesson, for instance by asking him a question. Or the teacher might ask Martin to help emphasize a key point: "Martin, say to the whole class clearly: One percent is always equal to one-hundredth."

The goal of this strategy is to avoid focusing on what is wrong. Rather than call attention to misbehavior, the teacher redirects energy to productive purposes, letting the misbehavior evaporate. Some examples:

Sam keeps giving opinions on class proceedings to a neighbor. The teacher says, "Sam, please make a note of any comments you have about this issue. Later I'd like you to share them all with me. Don't mention them now. I'd like to move ahead quickly now. But do note your comments so that you can show them to me later."

Two students are arguing too heatedly. The teacher says, "You two seem excited. Let's try some mental arithmetic. Kristen, make a guess which is larger, a third of a hundred or two dozen. Amy, do you agree? Here's one for you: What's five times thirteen? Take a moment and work it out on paper, both of you, and see if you are correct." The expectation is that the students will soon forget much of the heat of their earlier argument.

A student is strolling about, creating a distraction during quiet reading time. The teacher says, "Juan, please bring me that dictionary from the back before you sit and read."

THE CALM REMINDER

The purpose of the calm reminder is to remind students what they are supposed to do, in a way that does not communicate negative emotions. This strategy can be used at any time.

Even well-intentioned students forget. This is something I sometimes forget myself, and when I do I am apt to resent having to restate a requirement. Yet sometimes a calm reminder is the best choice. For a respectful class climate, a calm restatement is certainly better than a response that might bite or demean, such as "Were you paying attention the first time I said it?" or "Didn't I explain that already?" Here are two examples of calm reminders:

Nicholas, I'd like you to notice if the hall pass is on the hook before you ask about it.

Tom, when our hands go up, it's the signal to end small-group talk.

Rather than complain or fuss, I will sometimes just explain a procedure again, as if I had never said it before. No blame, just a simple restatement. The unspoken message: "I guess this didn't register in your memory." No big deal.

However, I do not always remind students of procedures. It takes a judgment about what is best in a particular situation. See the "once" principle presented in chapter 2 for a strategy that aims to eliminate unnecessary reminders.

THE NEXT-TIME MESSAGE

The purpose of the next-time message is to correct students' behavior without making them feel discouraged. The strategy calls for the teacher to tell students what to do next time, without focusing on what was done this time. The strategy can be used whenever the teacher finds it appropriate.

Teachers can invite guilt into the classroom by focusing on what has gone wrong. Moorman (1985) suggests that, when a correction is needed, the teacher talk not about this time but about next time. Some examples of the next-time message:

Nicholas, next time remember to put your paper in the box.
Sheila, next time please ask before you use my pencil.

Next-time messages are best delivered matter-of-factly. When I use them, I do not intend my tone to communicate, "You should know better." I do not want to focus on what was already done. I simply want to remind students what I think would be preferable for next time.

THE CHECK-YOURSELF MESSAGE

The purpose of the check-yourself message is to remind students to manage themselves responsibly. The strategy involves the teacher telling students to check what they have done, implying that when they do so they will see what corrections are necessary. The strategy can be used whenever students become careless.

Following are two examples of the check-yourself message in action:

Check yourself to see if the words are lined up properly on your paper.
Check to see if your notebook contains all five items.

Moorman (1985) also recommends check-yourself messages whenever students need a reminder. The intention is to avoid criticisim, and rather to imply "I know when you check you will see what to do. You are smart enough." Thus, teachers serve the objective of promoting intelligent self-reliance.

THE SILENT RESPONSE

The purpose of the silent response strategy is to give students room to solve their own problems. This strategy also provides a way of avoiding hasty, inappropriate responses. A teacher using this strategy reacts to an act of misbehavior by making a mental note only and considering later what, if any, action is appropriate. The strategy is appropriate when an act of misbehavior is not dangerous.

A student fails to bring in the required notebook, chats with a neighbor while the teacher talks, or neglects to do assigned work.

Pilon (1988) says that sometimes the best response is a silent response in which a teacher notes, "A problem here—let me keep it in mind and see, later, if something need be done and, if so, what."

Sometimes later attention is in fact needed. Yet sometimes the problem disappears on its own. That is especially likely if the class climate is becoming increasingly supportive and there is a growing respect for the teacher who, each time he or she responds silently to misbehavior, demonstrates sufficient poise not to be thrown off balance by every irritant in the day.

Responding to misbehavior by only making a mental note, not doing anything overt, is the response of a secure teacher, or a teacher wise enough to feign confidence until sufficient inner security does emerge.

When Not to Use the Silent Response

There are two instances in which I never recommend responding silently. The first is whenever physical danger is involved: A book is tossed across the room or a fight between students becomes more than playful. When physical danger exists, more than silence is called for. The second case is when the teacher's own mental health is imperiled. All teachers have their sore spots, behaviors that set off furies beyond their control. It is better in the long run, for both teachers and students, not to suppress those furies, not to bury insistent anger, not to amass lingering resentments. That is bad even for one's physical well-being. See the *honest "I" statement* (later in this chapter) for a strategy to address such situations.

Advantages of the Silent Response

Why respond to misbehavior only by making a mental note to oneself? After all, some experts tell teachers to act and act immediately in the face of misbehavior, before things get worse. However, as noted earlier, many problems disappear on their own. There's no sense in using energy to respond immediately to every incident or to respond when the act of misbehavior is not dangerous and might well solve itself or get solved by student initiative. Yet I do not recommend merely making a note of a problem when the motive is to avoid the discomfort of facing the problem. Students sense such timidity. Some tend to take advantage of it. At times like these, it's probably better to call on something like the simple authority statement.

The teacher who uses the silent response presents himself or herself as a personally secure adult, someone unworried that one incident will destroy the group. It can be reassuring and educational for students to have such a leader. In addition, working to be such a leader can increase one's own sense of peace and security.

The silent response communicates a confidence and trust in students, a confidence that they can and will learn to manage their own behavior, that they do not need to be babied, told what is right and what is wrong, always told what to do and what not to do. The silent response harnesses the power of positive expectations.

Often the silent response gives a teacher the space to choose what response would produce the best long-term effect. In a way it is a variation on the tried-and-true strategy of counting to ten before responding to an irritant. By contrast, the immediate, more impulsive response works against a teacher's larger purposes and limits his or her options.

Furthermore, an immediate response to a student who has just messed up adds awareness and energy to misbehavior. Teachers often do better to turn awareness and energy toward the behavior they want to see in the classroom, to accent the positive, not add attention to acts they would prefer to see forgotten. This is especially important in terms of any concern for student dignity and growth in self-management. When a student act is singled out for a teacher response, very often a student with questionable self-worth experiences a further weakening of self-worth. Very often the student feels inside, "I was bad," not, "The act was bad." Rarely does the student feel, "Perhaps I can learn something valuable about how to behave in the future."

Withholding an immediate overt response is not the same thing as no response at any time. I might note a behavior problem and then the next day teach or reteach a lesson to some or all of the class. For example, if I see too much aimless walking about, I might role-play walking in class with efficient purpose and respect for all, without criticizing any students for prior behaviors.

A junior high school teacher writes:

> I like the silent response. I use it all the time. If I had to react to each and every little disturbance both the students and I would go crazy. My first reaction is to ignore a problem. If I reacted every time someone disturbed the class I bet some students would only mess up *more* frequently, and get pleasure out of that.

My general preference is to intervene minimally. I believe in leaving enough space so students can practice and learn self-discipline. That requires that I remember to ignore minor disturbances, which actually makes things a lot easier for me and helps those students who are already prone to be hassled by adults, the ones likely to be oversensitive to criticism.

A high school teacher writes:

> Ginger was repeatedly late to my class, but only a few seconds late. At first it bothered me. Then I sensed Ginger was playing an independence game, that her style was not to go along with authority figures. She was bright enough so her lateness was not serious and it was not prompting others to be late, so I decided to ignore the issue and let her live her life in her way. Interestingly, when her lateness stopped bothering me, Ginger stopped being late. Odd, eh?

CLOCK FOCUS

The purpose of the clock focus strategy is to settle student restlessness and increase students' powers of concentration. The strategy calls for the teacher to announce "clock focus," a cue to students to stand and watch the second hand of a clock make full circles, as many rotations as they choose, and then to sit and resume their individual work. The strategy can be used whenever students need to be settled down, particularly young students working at individual tasks.

Sometimes an elementary school class will get restless, especially during long stretches of individual work. At such times I might announce, "Clock focus please." This is how one teacher explained this procedure to students on the first day of school:

> When I call "clock focus," here is what you do. You stand, relax, and then watch the second hand of the wall clock. Practice managing your attention. Practice your focus power. Just watch closely as the second

hand moves around the circle. You can watch for one full circle, or two, or three full circles, depending on how much focus power you want to practice. This develops your ability to concentrate. It's also good for settling yourself. You can do this anytime, whenever you want to settle your energies.

Let's try it all together now. Stand and do a clock focus for at least one full circle now and, whenever you are ready, sit and resume your work. We will practice this again later, but let's do it once now and then talk about how it went. Clock focus please!

Clock focus is another strategy I learned from Pilon (1988). I like it because it helps students get better at managing their energies and focusing their attention. It also develops powers of concentration. I suspect students like clock focus for another reason: It gives them a chance to stand and take a break from intense class work.

THE VISITOR'S CHAIR

The purpose of the visitor's chair strategy is to position a student close to the teacher without communicating disapproval. The teacher using this strategy asks a student to sit in a "visitor's chair" close to where the teacher is sitting or standing. Students know they can return to their own seats whenever they feel ready for responsible self-management. This strategy can be used when a young student needs proximity to the teacher and time to regain personal composure.

When young students are working individually, sometimes one student will talk too loudly or tease others or otherwise be disruptive. Often that problem will soon enough disappear; in such instances a silent response is the best approach. However, if the incident is seriously disruptive, or if it continues, the use of the *visitor's chair*, a term Pilon (1988) uses, might be in order. It might be introduced the first few days of the year, like this:

Sometimes, class, when we are scattered around the room, one or another of us is apt to lose our composure, talk too loudly, or somehow disturb others. When you notice you did something like that, put on the brakes quickly. Just stop it. No one is perfect. We all have impulses that can get us disturbing others. Be aware when that happens to you and stop it. That's practicing mature self-management.

If someone near you is disturbing others, and you see that the person is not aware enough or not self-managing enough at that time to stop it quickly, hold out a hand like this (flat, parallel to the ground), to signal them that it's time to settle down. That might help them become aware and settle down. Let's help each other that way. As one of our class signs says, "No one need do it all alone. We can accept and support one another."

If I notice that you are not settling down right away, I may come over to you, or ask one of your classmates to go to you, and say, "visitor's chair." Your job then is to come sit in a chair near me, wherever I happen to be, until you settle down, at which time you may go back to your place.

You may want to do some clock focusing while in the visitor's chair. Or, if I am working with a group, I might invite you to work along with us. In any case, you may decide to go back to your own place whenever you have managed yourself and settled down. No need to ask my permission. All of you are intelligent enough to decide that on your own.

Note that when I want someone to come sit near me in a visitor's chair I do not call out the student's name, "Charles! Visitor's chair please." Such a public announcement can dent dignity and bring on resentment. Either I go over and speak to the student quietly or send a messenger over with instructions to "speak quietly to Charles and ask him to come here."

If a student is not being dangerous to self or others and not being seriously disruptive, a silent response might be preferable. It is often the case that I am more annoyed by Charles than are his classmates. The lesson they might need to learn is how to keep at work when all is not entirely peaceful around them.

HONEST "I" STATEMENTS

The purpose of honest "I" statements is to communicate honestly with students without generating defensiveness or guilt. Honest "I" statements also help teachers model a valuable interpersonal skill. The strategy calls for the teacher to talk honestly about personal needs and feelings, making "I" statements, avoiding comments about what "you" did or "you" said. This approach is especially useful when upsetting feelings emerge.

Communication theory teaches that the impact of "I" statements is very different from the impact of "you" statements. Figure 3-2 has some examples of similar statements expressed in "I" and "you" modes.

"I" statements often lead to mutual understanding. "You" statements suggest blame and lead to arguments, resistance, social isolation, resentment, and retaliation.

Figure 3-2

"I" Statements versus "You" Statements

"I" statements	"You" statements
I hate it when I get interrupted! It makes me feel like what I say is unimportant.	You keep interrupting me! You have no respect for what I say. Stop doing that.
I'm angry about having to say the same thing three times! It's very frustrating for me.	I wish you would listen to me! You didn't hear me the first two times I explained.

"I" statements help students understand the effect their behaviors are having on others. They help students see the consequences of their acts in personal terms that they can understand deeply and clearly. "I" statements therefore are effective in showing students the natural consequences of misbehavior. They minimize the possibility that students will feel resentment or the urge to withdraw or retaliate. "I" statements maximize the possibility that students will want to cooperate and be supportive. It is wise, then, for teachers to become practiced at making "I" statements when misbehavior shows up.

It is also wise to teach students to make "I" statements. Here is how one teacher did:

> If a classmate does something that is disturbing to you, you might want to tell the person exactly what it is that is disturbing. Maybe the classmate was not aware of the impact of the behavior. You might say something like, "The tapping on your desk is really annoying to me right now. Maybe you didn't know that."
>
> If you absolutely *need* them to stop, tell the truth, tell them you need it. Learn to make honest "I" statements. Say something like, "I really need more quiet to concentrate and do my work."
>
> I call that an "honest 'I' statement." That is a statement that is *honest.* It says how you really feel or what you really want. And the focus is on *I:* what *I* feel, what *I* want—not on the other person, not on what *you* are doing or what *you* need to stop doing. "You" statements make people feel criticized and put down.
>
> I'd like this to be a class in which we are honest about our needs and in which we do our best to help people get what they need without put-downs. In the long run, we'll all get along better and appreciate each other's real needs if we learn to make honest "I" statements. We may not always be able to *do* what others want, but we can always respect others, and use our intelligence, and choose what is best to do.
>
> Let me role-play how this might go. I'll be a student now. I might say to a classmate, "What you're doing is bothering me. It's hard for me now to do what I want to do." That would be an honest "I" statement if it were true, if it was really hard for me to do what I wanted to do.
>
> Notice that I put the emphasis on what *I* want or need, not on what the other person was doing. I don't want to put others down or to treat them with less than full dignity. Blame often does that. Honest "I" statements make it easier for other people to under-

stand our situation without feeling blamed.

Let's pretend for a minute. Imagine someone was messing up your work. Write a sentence or two that first, would be honest, and, second, would not blame or complain but would be an "I" statement that talked about your own feelings or wants or needs.

Try it. Then we'll see if someone will risk reading what they wrote. Then we can work together, aiming to get all the potential blame out of each statement. Let's practice this a bit.

Ginott (1972) talks about a special advantage of using eloquence and variety when expressing feelings. We can enrich students' vocabulary and refine their emotional awareness when we use expressions such as "I'm feeling indignant," or "I'm chagrined," or "I feel bewildered, confused about what is best to do next."

Consider making a list of emotional words you would like your students to appreciate more fully. You might then review the list from time to time so that these words are available if and when a chance to use one comes up. Some possibilities: guilty, sorrowful, panicky, anguished, remorseful, suspicious, infuriated, depressed, awkward, fearful, anxious, glum, gloomy, ecstatic, irritated, manipulated, conflictful, regretful, heartache.

THE UNDONE-WORK RESPONSE

The purpose of the undone-work response is to respond wisely when students fail to do required work. The strategy involves the teacher avoiding a blaming response and instead aiming to create a growth-producing response. This approach can be used whenever a student has not completed work on time.

Students fail to do their work on occasion. Some students do not do their work on many, many occasions. Teachers can count on that as much as they can count on Monday mornings. My first recommendation is to treat such occasions as nonevents. Your students are simply doing what students always do and they would do it even if you were not you. When you must deal with students who fail to do what you asked them to do, remember that this is just part of your job, just another task to handle, just as you must handle lesson plans and grading.

My second recommendation is to avoid reacting in a way likely to do more harm than good. For example, I do not want to scold, use sarcasm, belittle, punish, or nag. That seldom works for long and, even when it does, is more likely to produce resentment or guilt than it is to lead to the kind of cooperative, responsible student I want. I certainly do not want students to withdraw from learning activities or conclude that I see them as defective persons.

In the long run, some reactions serve the interests of neither the teacher nor the student. Here are some examples:

- *Warnings.* "You know that if you don't do this you will suffer a more severe problem."
- *Punishments.* "Because you didn't do your work you must suffer by...."
- *Loss of learning chances.* "You cannot participate until you finish that work."
- *Loss of basic privileges.* "You lose out on fun or recess or being with others."
- *Involving parents.* "I want this work signed by your parents."

Here are some responses that are more likely to work in the long run:

- *Respectful reminder.* "Rich, please finish this paper later, before you start new work."
- *A "next-time" comment.* "Next time we have this work, please turn it in by the required time."
- *Inspiration.* "Come on, Kelly, let's do it! I know you can! Please let me be proud of you."
- *A sincere offer to help.* "Was it too difficult for you?" "Is there any way I can help you or get help for

you?" "How about doing just the parts you can do?" When using these questions, be sensitive to occasions when they could be taken as sarcastic or belittling.

- *A "natural consequence" discussion.* "You agreed to stay after school to finish that work, right? Since you didn't do it, certain results occurred. For example, I now have more difficulty trusting that you will do what you say you'll do. More serious yet, you may have difficulty trusting your own word. That is, it may have weakened your faith in yourself. What do you think about this?"
- *Acceptance.* "I don't know what else to say. I may have better ideas another time. Skip that requirement for now."

The basic issue is perspective. If teachers keep in mind that the goal is not only to teach subject matter but to do it in ways empowering to students in the long run, they are less likely to require work in ways that in the long run do more harm than good.

When in doubt, I prefer to do nothing. I want to avoid doing harm and instead back off from any confrontation and give myself time to find a constructive way to handle the situation.

Insisting for Inspiration's Sake

Sometimes I insist that work be done and, occasionally, for students who might need that kick, insist it be done right away. "You sit there and finish that page," I might say. Yet as I do that I want always to respect the dignity and self-management drives of students. I want to insist only in cases in which I sense that, deep inside, the student really wants to sit and do what is required but, just now, cannot do so without my insistence. Said another way, I want my insistence, when I do insist, to be inspiring, to bring out the best in students, not to be controlling, not to be denying, not to be disrespectful of the rights all people have to their own lives.

You might recall instances when someone insisted that you do something and, deep down, even if you resisted doing it, you knew it was good for you. The person was not demeaning you in any way. The person was, rather, challenging you to dig out more of your ability. The feeling of respect was there. When I insist that something be done, I want to be sure students know I am insisting for *their* welfare, not out of my stubbornness.

As teachers, we have much inherent authority, but we must not abuse that power. We do not want to insist that students fulfill requirements in ways that will slow their growth as responsible, self-managing students and citizens. We must handle requirements respectfully—and when we cannot do that, temporarily let go of requirements. Our aim is to serve good learning and good living.

THE SELF-ACCEPTANCE MONOLOGUE

The purpose of the self-acceptance monologue is to provide teachers a means of preserving their own peace of mind. The strategy calls for teachers to remind themselves that they should not expect to behave perfectly at all times. This approach can be used after one has acted less effectively than one would have wished.

Sometimes we don't live up to our own expectations. For example, you may not be in the habit of making "I" statements. You may prefer to make "I" statements but sometimes you notice that, once again, you failed to. Perhaps you fell back into a habit of complain and blame: "Why did you do that?" "You should know better than that." "You have to stop that." You, you, you.

"Ugh," you say to yourself, "why don't I say, 'I can't understand why that behavior continues,' 'I thought we had handled that,' or 'I need that to stop' ?"

What now? In the face of failure at that or any other preferred strategy, I recommend a firm self-acceptance monologue, which goes something like this:

Okay, I did it. It would probably have been better for the students if I had made an honest "I" statement or, if that was out of reach, had made a silent-note-only response and waited until I was more prepared. But I didn't. Again, I snapped out.

I don't want to focus on my weaknesses. I am not yet perfect. Might as well accept that. No sense in rejecting the part of me that is imperfect. Should I focus on the past act? No use. The question is what, if anything, I want to do the next time such a situation arises. So let's see, what can I do next time?

I want students looking at their inappropriate act without guilt, without resignation, without dismay. I want them to think about what happened and learn from it. I do not want them stuck in discouraging memories or obsessed with personal imperfections. I want them to feel confident about doing better. Ditto for their teachers.

I like sharing the self-acceptance monologue with students. Sometimes I tell students how I used a self-acceptance monologue—what I said to myself and why. That teaches a valuable life skill by modeling. Sometimes, after explaining the strategy to students, I ask if any of them have already talked that way to themselves and how it worked. Finally, I invite students to experiment with self-acceptance monologues and, if appropriate, to let the rest of the class know if it helped them in some way.

THE REALITY-ACCEPTANCE MONOLOGUE

The purpose of the reality-acceptance monologue is to help teachers "maintain sanity" when annoying behavior persists. The strategy calls for teachers to accept the fact that not all bothersome behavior can be eliminated and, when necessary, to remind themselves of that reality. This strategy is especially appropriate when nothing seems to work to improve a student's behavior.

Judy Kupsky, a teacher who tested some of these strategies for us, tells of a boy in third grade who was keeping her awake nights:

He was wired with high energy and no self-control. Nothing anyone could think to do had any effect. He kept calling out, moving about, bothering people around him, messing up the class. It was driving me crazy. The harder I tried to stop his disruptions the worse it got. Finally I gave up trying to change him. Like my stringy hair, I realized there was nothing to do but live with it as best I could. He just was not going to change. After I gave up, I realized the other students were not nearly as bothered as I was. Now somehow I don't expect him to change and I don't fight it and things are not nearly so bad. Fighting with it was the worst part. Now I have more energy to live with it.

Teachers assume that bothersome behavior should always be eliminated. When a teacher encounters a student whose behavior seems impervious to change, the teacher can all too easily become stuck in double frustration—frustration at the student's actions themselves, plus frustration at being unable to effect change in the student.

When this kind of frustration occurs, it often helps to remind oneself that we cannot always get things to turn out the way we want. It may be best to accept that reality and move on. In such instances a reality-acceptance monologue such as the following might help:

I realize I was assuming I could get him (or her, or them) to change. It looks like that won't happen, at least not now. No sense in continuing to fight that reality. Might as well accept it. Let me just deal with the reality as best I can now and stop worrying about trying to change it.

I suspect that most students have less difficulty adjusting to bothersome students than teachers do because students do not assume that they can change others.

For them, it's more a matter of how best to minimize the difficulties.

APOLOGIZING

The purpose of the apologizing strategy is to model a behavior important to the development of mature relationships. Apologizing also helps reduce feelings of guilt in the classroom. The strategy entails the teacher offering a brief apology and perhaps discussing the advantages of students also using apologies. The strategy is appropriate following actions that the teacher regrets having taken.

People in strong positions often feel that to apologize is to admit weakness. People in weak positions often feel that an apology only weakens them further. Yet an apology can be a forthright, caring "I" statement: "I did something that was hurtful to you and I'm sorry about that."

I often find it helpful to make apologies in the classroom. "I'm sorry," I might say, "that I nagged so much yesterday about neatness. I wish I hadn't done that. Now for today's lesson...." Just a simple statement often works wonders.

I also like to encourage students to learn the art of apologizing. With a high school class, I once said something like this:

> Class, I'd like to see us apologize when we make a mistake and hurt someone. As you will probably see, I will apologize from time to time. Sometimes I get too impatient, or too irritable, or too tired, or too something. And I snap at someone or, sometimes, the whole class. I may not realize that until later. Yet I like to come back and say I'm sorry once I get a better perspective.
>
> Let me show you what I mean. I once snapped at a student and the next day said, "I'm sorry when I got so angry and talked so irritably. No one deserves such treatment. I hope I didn't hurt your feelings. I don't want to hurt you or anybody else. It's just that some-

times I'm unable to do better. I'm sorry if I hurt you."

Sometimes I may say that to a whole class. And you too might apologize sometimes. It clears the air. It often dissolves guilt. It helps keep a group running smoothly. And usually it makes us all feel a bit closer.

To give us some practice now, please write down a few phrases you might use to apologize. Imagine that you made a mistake and acted in a way that was not your best self. Maybe start by imagining what you could say or do that might be hurtful to someone. Then write some words you might say the next day to that person. After a few moments, I'll ask you to share your ideas with a partner. Maybe someone would be willing to role-play such talk for us all. Let's see what we can learn about this.

Such a lesson is often unnecessary. I find that simply as a result of my modeling an apology, students pick it up and begin to apologize to each other more often. I find that that contributes substantially to a healthy feeling of classroom community.

One teacher comments on how modeling the apology can work even in preschool classrooms:

> Nowadays I go out of my way to apologize to my little tykes. Some of them only know scoldings and, too often, beatings. I doubt if some of them ever in their whole lives heard an apology from an adult. It's catching. Little Timmy the other day got angry and blasted some blocks that messed up others. Another boy was ready to hit him, I think, but Timmy said, "I'm sorry I did that," and immediately all seemed to have been forgotten.

THE WAITING PLACE

The purpose of the waiting place strategy is to provide a convenient place for a misbehaving student to wait before having a dialogue with the teacher. The strategy calls for the teacher to indicate a place where a student will be asked to wait until the teacher has time for a private conversation. The waiting place is most appropriate with young students, early in a course.

Young students can profit from having a special spot designated as a *waiting place.* A teacher using this strategy might say:

> Girls and boys, sometimes I find it useful to speak to a student privately, to tell about a prize or to give some personal advice. And sometimes I'll be too busy to do it right away. I'll want you to wait for me, so we can talk privately when I have a moment.
>
> For our waiting place, I'd like to use that corner, right near the door. Let's call that our waiting place. Victor, will you please go to the waiting place. A little further back, Victor. Yes, that's the spot.
>
> From now on, whenever I ask you to go to the waiting place, please stand over there and wait for me. You might do a clock focus while waiting. I'll try not to be too long. Then we can talk privately and you can go back to your work.

Soon after this strategy is introduced, it might be wise to ask a student to go to the waiting place. It is wise, too, to initially use the waiting place for events that are not of a disciplinary nature. The waiting place can be used, for example, when you want to send a message home with one child or give a private compliment to someone. Subsequently, it can be used whenever it would be valuable to have a student disengage briefly from classroom activities while the teacher is busy elsewhere. It can be used as a place where a student can take some time to settle down, or as a place to wait until the teacher can conveniently offer, say, a calm reminder, next-time message, or apology.

CHAPTER 4

Using Positive Intervention

THE BROKEN RECORD

The purpose of the broken-record strategy is to provide teachers with a means of asserting authority without arguing with students. The strategy calls for the teacher simply to repeat a statement that a student seems not to be respecting. The strategy is especially useful when a student is unaware that he or she is not hearing the teacher's message.

Canter and Canter (1976) talk about the "broken-record technique." Here is an example of this strategy in action:

Teacher: Alex, we do not fight in this room. I never want you to fight here again. I never want anyone hurt.

Alex: Peter started it. He hit me first.

Teacher: That might well be. I didn't see. But we don't fight in this room. Please remember that.

Alex: Well, Peter started it.

Teacher: Perhaps so. I'll watch in the future. But remember that we do not fight in this room.

Canter and Canter say that the broken-record strategy is especially effective when students do not seem to acknowledge a teacher's original statement. Charles (1992) reports two cautions provided by Canter and Canter: (1) When you repeat your original statement, preface it with a comment showing you heard what the student said: "That might well be," or "I understand your feeling." (2) Repeat your statement a maximum of three times to avoid slipping into a verbal power struggle with a student.

PERSON-TO-PERSON DIALOGUE

The purpose of person-to-person dialogue is to advance mutual understanding between teacher and student. When employing this strategy, the teacher engages in a private dialogue with the student, mainly using honest "I" statements. This strategy is especially useful when it appears that the student is not fully appreciating the teacher's perspective.

A person-to-person dialogue is a private talk between a teacher and a student. It is meant to be free of blame, rancor, and argumentation. The aim is mutual understanding.

Consider this example. Kara has been disrupting the class by persistently talking to her neighbors. Yesterday the teacher tried a simple authority statement: "I need you to be quiet during lessons. I find your talk to nearby students quite distracting." No luck. Today Kara keeps up her distractions, if anything more defiantly. The teacher asks Kara to talk with her in the hall while the rest of the students are busy at their desks.

Teacher: Kara, I must admit your talking is getting to me. I find it very hard to take. (Pauses.)

Kara: (Hangs head, watches feet, silently.)

Teacher: I'm not sure what to do, Kara. The situation is beginning to feel serious to me.

Kara: Well, stop picking on me.

Teacher: (Mildly) Seems like I'm picking on you . . .

Kara: Sure. You never look at others in the class who are talking too. Others talk just as much as I do.

Teacher: (Wanting to communicate that she understood what Kara said) The other students seem to talk as much as you.

Kara: Yeah. Right. (Kara seems to have nothing more to say.)

Teacher: I don't want to pick on you, or anyone else. I want to be fair to all my students.

Kara: Then stop picking on me!

Teacher: I'll try to watch that, Kara. I'm sorry if I did that. I wonder, though, if that will solve my problem. I mean I'm still worried that you'll talk to your neighbors during the lessons, distracting me and messing up the atmosphere I think is best for good learning in class. (She pauses, not wanting to make this into a lecture.)

Kara: Well, then stop picking on me.

Teacher: Yes, I'll try to make sure I don't do that. (Pauses.)

Kara: Can I go now?

Teacher: (Unsurely) Maybe we've talked enough for now. I guess you understand that it bothers me a lot when you talk to neighbors during lessons. And I understand that you don't want to be picked on. So let's leave it at that.

The conversation may not have accomplished much. But it probably did nothing to make the situation worse, as it might have if Kara felt dislike or rejection from the teacher. There is a possibility that the respect the teacher demonstrated toward Kara will make her feel more cooperative, more willing to curb her distracting talk. Such dialogues often have that effect.

It is not always easy to engage a disruptive student in a person-to-person dialogue. The chief danger is that the student will feel blamed and, as a result, will become defensive and resistant to future efforts to improve behavior. To avert that problem, I try not to assume that the conversation will solve the problem. I choose a more modest target: increased mutual understanding. I aim to talk in a way that communicates that no one is to blame. It is simply that a conflict exists between two sets of needs. In the above example, the conflict is between Kara's need to talk and the teacher's need for no talk.

A person-to-person dialogue can be used to bring different needs to the surface. The teacher might then trust that people's kindness and cooperative instincts will motivate an appropriate change of behavior.

I recommend against persisting if a conversation gets bogged down or keeps getting off track. I might simply disengage with a comment such as, "I don't know where to go from here. I'd like to put this conversation on the shelf for now and think about it more. Maybe we should talk together another time."

Here are four guidelines I recommend for person-to-person dialogues:

1. Make honest "I" statements about what is inside you. Avoid focusing on what the student does or does not do. Be truthful about your thoughts and, especially, feelings. Risk communicating your ideals, anxieties, frustrations, needs, and fears. Help the student see that you too are a feeling human being.

2. Defer to the student. Pause often. When the student wants to speak, stop and allow it. Don't give mini-lectures. Help the student see that you want to understand.

3. Every time the student speaks, show that you really heard. Perhaps pause for time to digest the words. Summarize what the student said. Repeat a few of the words the student used. Or just show attentiveness by nodding.

4. Avoid asking questions. Questions such as "Why did you do that?" or "Didn't you know I was bothered?" often make students feel controlled, manipulated, or defensive. Questions in disciplinary situations tend to make students feel inferior and accused. That reaction can be averted by turning questions into statements: "I'd like to know if you had a reason for what

you did." "I wonder if you knew I was bothered by what you were doing."

THE SELF-MANAGEMENT CONTRACT

The purpose of the self-management contract is to solve a discipline problem in a way that cultivates student self-responsibility and creates a win-win situation. The contract also shows students how interpersonal conflicts can be resolved peacefully. Three steps are involved in the strategy: (1) a person-to-person dialogue aiming for mutual student-teacher understanding, (2) brainstorming to produce a written list of possible steps to ease the problem, and (3) a review of the list to reach a mutual agreement about what might be done next. The strategy can be used whenever it seems to be needed.

The self-management contract strategy begins with a person-to-person dialogue, as described earlier in this chapter. It proceeds much further, however. Consider this example:

Teacher: Ethan, I asked you to talk with me because your restlessness in class is really getting to me. I see you talking out of turn and generally bothering the people around you. It's certainly distracting to me. I get the feeling you don't care to listen to my lessons. Today I even sensed, and I may be wrong, that you *enjoy* messing up the lessons, that you get pleasure out of it. Sometimes I even feel as if I'm being teased. That gives me very uncomfortable feelings. And I'm frustrated about what to do. I wonder if you can tell me anything about this.

This example illustrates step 1 in the self-management contract strategy: *The teacher makes an honest "I" statement of feelings, thoughts, or needs.*

Often step 1 is sufficient. The key is to be honest and show the student that you too are a feeling, needful person. Often a student will respond to such an honest statement more or less apologetically and thereafter behave more or less satisfactorily. But not always. Here is how the discussion with Ethan might proceed if step 1 is not sufficient:

Ethan: It's not always my fault. David does the same thing and you don't notice him!

Teacher: I understand, Ethan. It seems like I'm ignoring David. But I want to talk about my concerns with your self-management now. I wonder if you would be willing to practice better self-control.

Ethan: (After a pause with the teacher simply waiting) I'm not that bad. What do you want me to do, anyhow?

Teacher: Well, I guess the main thing that bothers me is the way you move about and distract me and I suspect distract others during a lesson. I really need you to practice controlling that better.

Ethan: I'm just kinda restless. I like to move. David does the same thing and others too and you never pick on them.

Teacher: Perhaps, but I wonder if you would be willing to consider making a plan to control yourself better.

Ethan: What do you mean?

Teacher: Well, let's brainstorm a minute. Let's list some things you *might* do that could get you to handle your restlessness better during lessons. Let's just imagine and list some ideas for now. Later we can go back and see if any of the ideas are worth a try. For example, you might put a reminder sign on your desk, maybe saying "Relax." I'll write that on this paper as number one. (Pause as teacher writes, "1. Reminder sign on desk.") Or maybe you could ask a neighbor to signal you every time you get restless and don't notice it yourself, so you could pull yourself together and settle down. I'll list that as idea number two: "Ask neighbor to remind me." Any ideas you can think of?

Ethan: Nah. David needs to be here too, you know.

Teacher: I might have to talk to David sometime, but now, let me think. For three, you could talk this over with a friend, tell a friend how I said that this behavior was bothering me. See if that turns up any good ideas. I'll write number three, "Talk it over with a friend." Any other possibilities come to mind?

Ethan: Nah. I guess I could walk around some. That might help.

Teacher: That's an idea. (Writes: "4. Walk around.") (Long pause) Maybe I could make up a special signal for you when I need you to settle down, like touch my left ear.

Ethan: Nah. I don't want any special signals. David and some others need that too, you know.

Teacher: OK. But now we're just brainstorming and we want to write all the ideas we can dream up. Later we can see if we both agree some are worth trying. Let me write that so I don't forget it. (Writes: "5. Special signal to settle down.")

Ethan: I could quit this class.

Teacher: That's another idea. (Writes: "6. Quit this class.") Any other ideas?

Ethan: Nah.

That example illustrates step 2 of the self-management contract strategy: *The teacher starts a brainstorming session to produce a list of possible actions to improve the situation.* All ideas are to be accepted, and—this is critical—all ideas are to be written down. In the process, all student comments are to be acknowledged. The teacher might paraphrase student comments or say "I understand," much as the teacher did in the example when Ethan mentioned David. The students must know that the teacher listens to them, just as the teacher wants to be listened to. Give students plenty of time to talk. Do not give mini-lectures. Pause often.

Avoid asking questions. Instead, make statements. Rather than ask, "What can you do about your restlessness?" state what is on your mind: "I wonder if you have any ideas about what you can do" or "If you have any ideas, please let me know." When a teacher turns questions into statements, and then pauses so that the student has an opportunity to respond (or not respond), student defensiveness is reduced, and, more important, the teacher demonstrates a respect for the student's capacity to manage his or her own life.

After the brainstorming list is developed, step 3 is often needed: *The teacher and student review the list to reach an agreement on a specific action plan.*

> **Teacher:** Maybe we'll think of more ideas to write down later, but let's see if we think any ideas on this list are worth trying. Let's look at this sheet together. I'd be willing to go along with numbers one and three. (Teacher puts a check mark by those.) And I guess I'd go along with number two. (Checking that too.) Any of those you would agree to go along with?
>
> **Ethan:** I'd agree to try one, maybe. And four.
>
> **Teacher:** Well, we both agree on number one, "Reminder sign on desk." Let's try that for a few days. Maybe we can think of some other ideas to try later. But, for number one, let's be specific now and work out the details.

Sometimes several follow-up discussions will be called for. These might reinforce or adjust the action plan. Follow-ups are especially appropriate for students who have unusual difficulty managing emotions or impulses, or who do not expect respectful treatment from teachers, or who are accustomed only to rewards and punishments and do not respect their potential for learning to manage their lives intelligently. Here is a sample follow-up, in which the teacher holds the student to his agreement:

> **Teacher:** I didn't see a sign on your desk today.
>
> **Ethan:** I can't find it. Maybe the cleaning people threw it away.
>
> **Teacher:** Ethan, we agreed you would keep a reminder sign on your desk.
>
> **Ethan:** I know, but it got lost.
>
> **Teacher:** What was our agreement?
>
> **Ethan:** OK, OK, I'll make a new one. You sure are pushy!
>
> **Teacher:** (Ignoring Ethan's remark) Thanks, Ethan. See you later.

A self-management contract can be the best means to teach a difficult student an especially meaningful lesson: that at least one adult knows that he can learn to live as an intelligent, self-managing citizen and, furthermore, that one adult cares enough to take the time to help him or her do that. It is, for some students, a sobering, heartening lesson.

Does agreement on a plan always emerge? Do students always follow through? No and no. Yet many teachers find that the process itself drains the heat from problems. Many problems cease being serious, perhaps because the process provides a better understanding of the student and therefore enables the teacher either to accept the behavior or find new ways of handling it. It is also possible that the contract process helps students become more cooperative because it helps them understand and appreciate the teacher's concern and respect for them.

How strongly should a teacher press students to control impulses? Strongly enough to communicate that you trust that they can achieve self-control if and when they choose to do so, but not so strongly that you communicate that they must achieve self-control now, whether they are ready or not and whether they choose to or not, as if their dignity and readiness for self-management were of no moment. Take care not to get into a power struggle with students. It is better to wait for another time and another opportunity than to try to break a student's will.

WHOLE-CLASS PROBLEM SOLVING

The purpose of whole-class problem solving is to get maximum input for solutions to a problem and maximum commitment to chosen actions. The strategy also enables the teacher to model a mature problem-resolution strategy. Two steps are involved in the strategy: (1) the class brainstorms and produces a written list of possible solutions and (2) the class reviews the list to develop an action plan that is acceptable to both teacher and students. The strategy is especially appropriate when a problem involves a large portion of the class.

The steps in the self-management contract strategy can be applied to whole-class issues such as what to do when too many students are late, how to handle cliques, what to do when the heating system fails to keep the class warm enough, or how to help students who are falling behind. An episode of whole-class problem-solving might begin with the following statement by a teacher:

> Class, before we get going today I'd like to talk about the problem we've been having with class supplies. As I once mentioned, I don't like waste. I wonder if we could brainstorm possible ways to handle this better. Can I get two volunteers to write ideas on the board? OK, you two take turns writing all the ideas we come up with. Later, we'll go through the list. I'll see which ones I can live with, and we'll see which ones you all could live with. Our goal will be to create something that works for us all. But now let's be imaginative and see how many possible ideas, even ones that might seem a little strange or funny, we can list that might help us with this issue.

The whole-class problem-solving strategy tends to uncover more solutions than a teacher alone can dream up. It elicits student cooperation in the solution of the problem. It strengthens a sense of the class as community. It also models an effective way to solve social problems.

THE CONFLICT-RESOLUTION LESSON

The purpose of the conflict-resolution lesson is to teach students how to solve problems in a nondestructive, mutually respectful way. When using this strategy, the teacher shows students how to talk honestly about a conflict and, if talk alone does not ease the conflict, how to brainstorm and write a list of possible next steps. This strategy can be used whenever the teacher feels that the time has arrived for students to improve conflict-resolution skills.

Some elements of the strategies presented earlier in this book can be used to teach students how to handle their own conflicts. A first-grade teacher used honest "I" statements for this purpose, in this way:

Let's say someone kept messing up your toys, or kept teasing you or otherwise made you angry. What can you do? You could scream or hit or cry. But there is a more intelligent way to react.

Let's say a boy, we'll call him James, keeps pushing to the front of the line. And let's say you get very angry at that. You might go up to him and say, "James, I don't like it when you don't wait your turn. I get mad when you push in the line."

You might say that after James pushed into line. Or if that was not a good time to talk, you might wait until later. "James," you might say, "I want you to know that when you push in line like you do at the water fountain, I don't like it. It makes me mad."

You don't have to do more than that. Just tell James the truth about how you feel. Maybe he didn't know he was causing such bad feelings. Maybe he would be willing to cooperate better if he knew that more people were getting upset.

That's a healthy way to settle conflicts. What you do is make what we call "honest 'I' statements." We just tell the person honestly how we feel. The idea is not to hurt the other person or make that person angry. It's just to get the feelings out, so the other person knows, and so we don't have to keep bad feelings locked inside us.

Let's try acting out a situation. Let's say someone took your pencil and didn't give it back. And that made you angry. Who would be willing to play a person like that? Thank you, Lisa. Who would be willing to act out the person who took the pencil? OK, Holly, you stand there. Lisa, over there so we all can hear. Now imagine Holly has your pencil, Lisa. Go over to her and simply tell her the truth about how you are feeling.

Several trials might be valuable, as well as a follow-up role-play another day. Especially valuable are follow-up questions: "Who can remember what I said about a healthy way to handle conflicts when they come up?" or "Who can tell me what I mean by an honest 'I' statement?" or "Anyone use an honest 'I' statement in the last few days? Are you willing to tell us about it?"

I like showing students that I too am a feeling human being. One way I do that is to give examples from my own life, perhaps when introducing this conflict-resolution model, or perhaps as a review:

> I used an honest "I" statement with my neighbor the other day. In his house they play music too loud and too late into the night and we can hear it. Sometimes it's hard to sleep. I mentioned it to my neighbor last week, just telling him that we were having trouble with the loud music. I asked if he wouldn't mind turning it down. But nothing changed and I was getting very upset.
>
> So I told him. I called him up and said, "I'm getting very upset over here. When I hear music from your house my blood pressure zooms up high. My family is getting upset with me because I'm getting too nervous and I just wanted you to know how serious a problem that is for me."
>
> That's about all I said. It was an honest "I" statement. The neighbor said he'd try to keep the sound lower. It seems lower, but it's too soon to tell. An honest "I" statement does not always solve a conflict between people. But it's a lot easier and safer than fighting or suffering endlessly. I wanted to share that example from my own life.

A second-grade teacher writes:

> I was not sure what to expect but I thought I'd try teaching my second graders the honest-"I"-statement way to resolve conflicts. We talked about conflicts in life and about fighting and war and laws against hurting others and even the United Nations. Then I said they themselves have conflicts and we role-played a

situation in which a brother kept changing the TV channel and the sister was getting angry. Instead of hitting or complaining to a parent, the sister, quite coolly I thought, said how she felt to the brother. I asked the students to guess how the brother felt when he heard that. The class concluded that the brother would have felt lots worse if he had gotten in trouble with his parents. Anyhow, the next day one boy said he used an honest "I" statement when an uncle changed the TV channel while he was watching a program he was allowed to watch. He said it worked! And I think a girl on the playground used it the other day, but I'm not sure about that. I'll bet there will be fewer arguments and fights in this group.

A high school counselor writes about applying the three steps of the self-management contract strategy to interpersonal problems:

We began using our detention room for lessons on good living. Last week I had the best lesson in a long time. I taught them how to make honest "I" statements when they were in conflict with each other and how to negotiate differences when honest talk alone didn't solve the problem. I used a three-step model: (1) Initiate person-to-person dialogue about the conflict. (2) If the conflict remains, write a brainstormed list of possible resolutions. (3) Go back over the list and try to agree on some resolutions to try. As we talked about this and role-played this model, it was clear to me that no one in the room (there were about fifteen students) had any idea conflicts among themselves could be resolved in nondestructive ways.

DRAMATIC DISTRACTION

The purpose of the dramatic distraction strategy is to keep behavior problems in the classroom from getting worse, and to allow time for the positive energies of students to come forth. The strategy calls for the teacher to turn attention forcefully away from problem behavior to something more healthful, such as a safe venting of feelings, or to something nonemotional, such as a math puzzle or riddle. This approach is especially useful in situations too tense for reasonable resolution.

Dramatic distraction resembles the redirect-energy strategy, but it is much more dramatic. For example, when a teacher confronts two boys who are fighting, the teacher does not touch either but speaks loudly, authoritatively, and insistently to both:

> Rob, put that hand down. Move over there. Right there! Charles, sit down right where you are. Sit right down! Rob, in a minute I'll ask you what's behind this. First, Charles, I want you to tell me what's going on!

Charles blames, threats, whines, complains, and groans. Rob does the same. But no matter. Teachers who intervene with a force of personality often get fighters to pause long enough to allow a verbal venting to begin. I call that a *dramatic distraction* because it begins by distracting students from the battle at hand.

Often it does not matter at all what the students say about the fight. When people get off balance enough to fight, they can rarely explain what is going on. What's important here is that the teacher got the students shifting hostile energies from punches to words. It is unnecessary—and in the long run, counterproductive—to apportion blame. After the teacher senses that enough energy has gone out of the fight, she might simply announce:

> OK, both of you. Get back to your work. We don't want people here acting out angry feelings like that. We all get upset. But intelligent people learn to manage upsets so they don't do serious damage. Both of you, pull yourselves together. We want to be together here as one community. Now move on.

In a second example, the teacher has to move between two fighting students and push them apart. She does not know either by name:

"You," she says, facing one boy, "Count backwards from 100 by twos. Go!" Mumbled responses.

"You," says the teacher, turning to face the other boy, "Count by threes, starting with ten. Go!"

Those odd demands, probably coupled with something inside the students that prefers to end the fight if they can only do so without losing face, does the job. The fight stops and the teacher sends the students on their way.

In a third example, a group of six-year-olds brings Debra to the principal's office.

"She was stamping on our feet, hard," several students complain.

"I see," says the principal. "Well, Debra, would you like to apologize to these boys and girls?"

"No," insists Debra, head down, eyes hard.

"Well, boys and girls, Debra is not ready to apologize now. Maybe another day. Before you all go back, who can count from two to twelve by twos? Anyone?"

The principal can be said to have ended that conflict by distracting students. Perhaps he has assumed that the time is not right for deeper healing or a long-term remedy. In any case, it is noteworthy that the principal does not agree that Debra did wrong or say something like, "We do not want people to be hurt like that, Debra. Please don't do that again." Such a statement would likely not register meaningfully.

The above incident occurred in one of Pilon's Workshop Way® schools. In talking about it, Pilon (Personal communication, May 7, 1993) says:

Students *do* have common sense. They do know what's right. And they *know* they know what's right. Scolding, even frowning, sends a very different message. It tells them I do not believe they know what's right. I never want to get students to doubt themselves that way.

In the incident with Debra, the principal probably avoided adding to Debra's negative self-concept. Debra may even have learned that a responsible adult trusts her to know right from wrong and appreciates that, at the moment, she is simply unable to behave in ways that reflect her intrinsic goodness. If so, it will likely inspire her to discipline herself and, of course, the approach here aims to inspire discipline.

Later on, of course, the principal can think about what else might be done to help Debra grow toward better self-discipline. There is no reason why all problems must be solved in one visit to the principal's office.

COOL-QUICK-CERTAIN CONTROL

The purpose of the cool-quick-certain control strategy is to ensure physical safety when one or more students become dangerously out of control. The strategy calls for the teacher to take control promptly and forcefully and as unemotionally as possible.

Occasionally a teacher will have to deal with a student who is completely, even dangerously, out of control. In a preschool class, Stephen jumps and runs about wildly. He heeds the teacher's loud insistence that he sit down only for a moment, if he bothers to listen to her at all. In junior high, Melanie is completely disrespectful. Ask her to lower her voice and she sneers bitterly. Ask her to stop poking Sarah and she gives a harder poke and then glares.

Here are three guidelines to help teachers deal with such situations:

Be cool. Do not show hostility. Act as unemotionally as possible.

Try not to resent the behavior. Treat students who are out of control as persons who are out of control—rather than as persons who are consciously trying to cause hurt. Just as a parent does not blame an infant with a pained stomach for crying, a teacher should not place blame on students who are thrashing about without self-control. Besides, blame invites resentment, which will make future interactions harder. Blame also invites self-condemnation, a hardening of any conclusion that "I am not a good person." When responding to a student who has gotten out of control, simply attempt to take action as coolly as possible, as you might if your car started going into a skid on a slick road.

> *Be quick.* Act quickly, especially if someone's safety is at stake. There will be time for more subtle, thoughtful approaches later.

Do not do anything to communicate that a student's out-of-control behavior might be permissible. If the student has exceeded safe limits, act promptly, even if you are unsure your limits are fair. You can always apologize later, which might bring you and the student closer. And you can always expand limits later, if you realize that your limits were unreasonable. You cannot tighten limits without inviting resentment, which will only make future interactions harder.

> *Be certain.* Act with confidence. Communicate that you mean what you say. Request specific actions.

Do not make demands related to a student's emotions, such as "Control your temper!" or "Explain your motives!" Such requests are difficult for students to fulfill. Ask for a physical action: "Sit in this chair by me." "Stand up and come with me." Or, use a dramatic distraction: "Count backward by threes from fifty-seven." "Do you remember the name of the capital of Pennsylvania?" Do not nag, whine, or scold. Do not punish or otherwise add to the student's pain. Provide the controlling force the student momentarily lacks. Act to stop the behavior.

There is an art to defusing an out-of-control situation, an art that teachers are best positioned to demonstrate when they are being their confident selves. There is also an art to distinguishing what is too dangerous from what—no matter how uncomfortable it makes one feel—is not too dangerous. Although there are no clear-cut rules for making this distinction, some behaviors are clearly serious enough to require immediate intervention. I would put into this category any behavior that endangers the physical safety of people.

Some behaviors might best be handled later, when tempers have cooled, perhaps with a special lesson for the class or for a limited group of students. I would put into this category acts that are not physically dangerous and that might in fact provide the basis for important lessons on how to live in a community—for example, students leaving a mess on the floor.

Teachers' personal boundaries will shift as they themselves change—and as students change—and as different groups show different needs and maturity levels. Teachers may also choose to accept certain limits because these limits are demanded by administrators or parents. I would however not recommend doing so if, as sometimes happens, we receive requests that we professionally judge not to be in the best interests of our students. All in all, we must draw our own limits. The core criterion question I use: What will best serve the current and long-term interests of us all?

THE CALAMITY PROCEDURE

The purpose of the calamity procedure is to reassert control of a classroom that has slipped into chaos. The strategy calls for the teacher to call out questions rapidly and forcefully and to direct students to write down the answers.

Sometimes a whole class can use a dramatic distraction. For such times, which Pilon (1988) calls "calamities," Pilon recommends that teachers keep on hand several sets of questions they can use to capture students' attention. For example, imagine that a teacher has just walked into a chaotic room. She speaks forcefully:

> Everyone. Take out a piece of scrap paper and write the number one. (Very short pause) Look in your

English text, on page 45. Write the last three words on that page.

There is a short pause as the teacher writes on chalkboard: "1. under the stars." There is no discussion and no expression of concern that most students have not yet moved to find their texts. The teacher assumes that the students will follow and moves right along:

Write the number two. On page 26. Write the four-word subheading in the middle of the page.

The teacher pauses and writes on the board: "2. No one ever knows." Again, with no discussion the teacher quickly moves on:

Write the number three. On page 104. Write the first three words of the first full paragraph.

And so it goes—rapid-fire directions to students to write the next question number, find the called-out page, and hunt for and then copy the material indicated:

Write number four. Page 35. Write the caption under the picture.

Write number five. Page 190. Write the names of two people mentioned in the second full paragraph.

Write number six. Page 12. Write the first word on that page that rhymes with "river."

Write number seven. The title page. Write the full name of the author.

Write number eight. Page 87. Write the place where whales were hunted in 1911.

Write number nine. Back pages of the book. Write true or false. There is no index in the book.

Write number ten. Page 122. Write the full name of the man pictured on the opposite page.

After calling out each question, the teacher pauses a beat and then writes the correct answer on the board. The tone is firm enough to catch up some students at the outset. As the procedure goes on and there is less for other students to do, more and more students join in. Students see that simply by paying attention and moving smartly they can write correct answers, experience success. By the time ten questions are finished, the teacher can expect the class to be somewhat settled, fairly balanced, ready to move on. "Fine," the teacher might say at the end, "please put that away and let's begin our review of yesterday's work."

No criticism. No complaints. Just a fast-paced procedure to channel the energies of the class into something they can handle.

Pilon suggests that ten questions be used, for it sometimes takes that many for the teacher to secure the involvement of the whole class. It seems to me that if the questions are less trivial, fewer than ten might do the trick. A single question might even do it, if it served to capture and hold student attention. Here is one example, reported by special education teacher Bruce Maskow:

> The room was in an uproar when I came in and I didn't even know why. But I knew I had to do something so I yelled, "Everyone sit down and start writing pairs of rhyming words. Go!" I called that out a few times because that class liked inventing simple rhymes and as some students actually began doing it, which surprised me, actually, I went over to the students I thought might do it next if I looked them straight in the eye. Finally I was able to get all but one girl sitting and at least thinking about writing. She was furious with another girl for flirting with her boyfriend.

TEMPORARY REMOVAL

The purpose of the temporary removal strategy is to obtain a respite from a problem situation. The strategy calls for the teacher to instruct a student to leave the group. This strategy is appropriate to use when it seems that no other strategy will work.

Although it is sometimes appropriate to ask a student to sit in the back of the room or wait in the hall, I recommend that only as a last resort and a temporary measure. I find that neither the student expelled from the group nor the class as a whole is likely to get long-term benefit from such an approach. Sometimes, however, there seems to be no choice. A student can get too far out of control, too close to injuring himself or others, or simply be too upsetting to the teacher.

When I separate a student from peers, my aim is to find a way to get the student back into classroom activities as soon as possible. "I wish I knew what to do," I have said to a student, whom I had earlier sent from class, continuing on, something like this:

> I want you to be with all of us in the classroom community, but I can't accept those disturbances. I'll think about what we can do to get you back in. Please, you do so also. If you are certain you can come back comfortably, maybe for a short time, let me know. I once had a student who came in and then, when he knew he would lose his self-control, went away from the group again. It was a self-managed system. Let me know if you want to try that. I'll talk to you later and see where we go from here. Let me say again that I'm sorry I can't now think of a better way to handle this situation. I really do wish I knew some way you could be in the middle of the group without my worrying about disturbances.

That is the kind of statement I would like to hear if I were that student.

What's important here is the aspect of the teacher that is being expressed. Is the teacher being punitive, hostile? Manipulative, self-serving? If so, I would not predict long-term success. Or is the teacher being honestly regretful and uncertain about what to do? Or perhaps being his or her open self, showing honest concern for the student? If so, long-term positive results are certainly possible.

Sometimes a long pattern of serious disruptive behavior exists and the student is best put in a special class. The primary objective of such classes should be to help students get back into the regular classroom community. I would not want to isolate such students any longer than necessary. I side with those who consider separation inherently unfair.

A special education teacher says:

> We have a signal. When I point to a student and say, "Out please," he knows it's time to stand outside the door. He also knows I am not intending to punish him. It's not a punishment for misbehavior. I often tell the class that we have no punishments here, that I do not believe punishment helps any of us in the long run. I therefore say "out" coolly, without any scold in my voice. The student then stands outside and knows that he can come back in the room anytime he thinks he has himself under control. I told the class, "You are all intelligent persons and able to know when it will be all right for you to return to your work." Students seem to appreciate my respect for their intelligence. That's the only way I use "time out" and it works very well for me.

THE POSITIVE PARENT SCHEDULE

The purpose of the positive parent schedule is to increase family support for students. The strategy calls for the teacher to prepare a schedule that makes it easy to give positive messages to all parents. This strategy is most effective when used early in the school year.

Some teachers make a schedule for giving positive comments to families about their children. One teacher takes the second weekend after school has opened to phone every family with a quick message, something like this:

> Mrs. Jones, this is Bill Schmidt, Tom's teacher, and I want to take a few seconds to let you know I am delighted with how Tom's been participating in our class. I don't want to take too much of your time right now, but I just wanted to be sure to tell you that you

can certainly be very proud of your son. Please say hello to him for me. Talk to you later. Goodbye.

"I've learned to expect," this teacher says, "that the parent will soon ask Tom what on earth he did that was so good. And that Tom himself will wonder. Often students ask me why I called. I just say that I want parents to appreciate their children (which some parents fail fully to do), and in fact that I'm delighted with how each of them has been handling the class so far. I don't make more of it than that and it works just fine."

Other teachers address a postcard to each family, watch for a specific act they appreciate, note it on the card and send it out, being sure to get all the cards sent before each month ends: "Just a card to say I appreciated the way (student's name)"...

• reached out to help someone without a partner today.

• comes on time every day ready to work. Shows real responsibility.

• had a beautiful happy smile when he walked in this morning.

• is willing to risk sharing his answer even when he might be wrong.

• helped clean up today.

Teachers who want students to be happy in their classrooms are wise to help students be happy in their homes.

DIAGNOSING STUDENT MOTIVATIONS

The purpose of diagnosing student motivations is to explore what might be motivating a student to keep misbehaving. In using this strategy, the teacher considers alternative reasons for a student's behavior and, when appropriate, makes a plan to lead the student toward more responsible patterns. This strategy is appropriate when a student chronically misbehaves.

Learning what motivates the behavior of a persistently troublesome student can sometimes help a teacher reduce disruptive behaviors. Dreikurs (1968) has described three motives for persistent misbehavior: *attention, power,* and *revenge.*

Attention motivates some students. They thirst to be heard, noticed, recognized. They sometimes talk a lot and loudly, or ask bothersome questions, or move about intrusively. A few greatly prefer negative attention to no attention at all and will cause trouble until they get sufficiently noticed. When a teacher feels annoyed by a student, it is often because that student is driven to get attention.

How can a teacher reduce the desire for attention? Not by forcing the student to be quiet; that rarely helps. When a student is being bothersome, my immediate response might be to use respectful reminders, respectful expressions of disapproval, clock focus, or the visitor's chair. In the long run, I recommend helping the student get more healthful experiences of being noticed. This can be done by means of support groups, learning pairs, cooperative-learning activities, and responding to needy students before they call for attention.

I also look for chances to help students learn preventative measures for self-control by using intelligence call-ups and self-management contracts and by teaching students how to make "be" choices.

I also seek ways to provide more healthful attention to students with behavior problems. For example, I arrange for them to tutor in other classrooms or become involved in group activities outside of school. In some cases, a home situation can be modified, as when students are too often alone at home.

Power motivates other students. Some students who exhibit troublesome behaviors are driven by a need for power, a need to exert control. Often the motive will derive from an irrational fear that harm might result if they do not control matters, as if an inner voice were saying, "If I'm not in charge, I don't know what will happen." Such students are sometimes furiously defiant. When a teacher feels threatened by a student, it is often because the student is driven by this need to control.

How can a teacher ease such a drive inside students? Not by engaging in a power struggle; that rarely helps. When incidents occur, a more effective response is to defuse passions by means such as cooling-off periods, dramatic distractions, temporary removal, clock focus, and the visitor's chair.

For the long run, I recommend aiming to help students feel safe by (1) using classroom procedures that are steady and secure, (2) providing frequent reminders about your own good intentions, (3) using the whole-self lesson to explain why all people sometimes act in nonpreferred ways and why it is wise to accept such actions, and (4) making frequent referrals to classroom signs, especially the signs about time clocks and group acceptance.

I also recommend aiming to strengthen students' appreciation of the need to learn self-control, by means such as honest "I" statements, intelligence call-ups, lessons on community living, respectful reminders, and self-management contracts. Also consider healthful ways for students to vent their need for power, such as recreation activities and opportunities to tutor slower students and engage in appropriate sports or hobbies. In some cases the power of the whole class can be healthfully marshaled, for example by whole-class problem solving: How can we help Patrick grow in self-management?

Occasionally a home situation can be modified to help the student, as when parents mistakenly assume punishments are helping the child or when they severely restrict a child's activities.

Revenge motivates other students. Some students seem intent on doing harm. They may damage property or tease others. Sometimes it seems as if they are paying back the world for pains they once experienced, and sometimes those pains can be identified. Yet sometimes no cause for destructive impulses can be found. When a teacher feels hurt by a student, it is often because that student is motivated by a desire for revenge.

How can teachers help students with vengeful impulses? Overlooking actions or delaying responses rarely helps the student, and it often leads to further harmful acts. Punishment is also rarely helpful because it typically fuels the impulse to do harm. Prompt, assertive, nonpunitive reactions (such as respectful disapprovals, honest "I" statements, the visitor's chair, and temporary removal) are more appropriate.

In the long run, I recommend aiming to reduce inner emotional pain and increase self-acceptance and acceptance by others by using whole-self lessons, cooperative learning, activities that increase a sense of classroom community, and strong demonstrations that the teacher remains accepting of all students, even while not accepting certain behaviors.

Also consider encouraging humor as a safe vent for hostile emotions and vigorous exercises or high-energy sports as safe vents for excess physical energies. In some cases a home situation can be modified, such as when a student is being abused at home.

PARENT AIDES

The purpose of having parent aides is to strengthen the adult presence in a classroom and increase school-parent cooperation. The strategy calls for the teacher to invite parents or other adults to visit often, perhaps to act as teacher aides. The strategy can be used at any time.

Some students who will readily misbehave if there is one adult in the room will rarely do so when two adults are present. Perhaps it is the extra pair of eyes, or the lack of a single focus for their authority-figure resentments, or the added mature presence in the room. Whatever the reason, having other adults in the classroom can reduce behavior problems.

There are other reasons to welcome parents, grandparents, or other adult visitors. For one, doing so creates an opportunity for publicity for good education; public criticism of schooling might diminish if more adults saw how hard teachers work. Having adults serve as aides can also bring parents closer to their children; parents can share in their children's daily experiences and perhaps get in a better position to help their children with homework. Perhaps most important, parents can see an adult interacting respectfully and productively with children, an experience that might have a positive effect on their parenting efforts.

Besides, adults can be valuable aides. One teacher sends a letter home to parents inviting them to visit anytime, without prior arrangements. She also sends an announcement to nearby service clubs soliciting volunteer aides. Whenever an adult shows up, a student monitor is instructed to give the visitor a sheet of visitor guidelines. It consists simply of a note of welcome and a list of suggested ways to help ("Just sit and enjoy watching the children," "Offer to help me assist individual students," "Join in at clean up time," "Offer to run errands," etc.) and suggested things to avoid ("Avoid giving special attention to your own child" and "Avoid assisting students who would do better to solve problems on their own").

THE DISCIPLINE SQUAD

The purpose of the discipline squad is to give teachers who feel physically vulnerable adequate feelings of security. The strategy involves having the teacher arrange for several other educators in the building to respond in times of emergency. The strategy might be used when teachers feel too threatened to work effectively.

Some teachers in some schools feel so threatened that calm, confident teaching is not possible. Canter (1989) suggests that such teachers might consider asking three or four other teachers or administrators to be ready, when called, to come immediately to help handle extremely difficult situations, such as when one or more students become unmanageably violent. The wisdom of this strategy is that it can allay the anxieties of a teacher to the extent that the teacher feels secure enough to handle problems alone and, therefore, rarely if ever needs to summon the discipline squad.

The risk involved in using the discipline-squad strategy is that it might undercut students' respect for a teacher's authority. When the problem situation is so extreme that students can see clearly why one adult alone could not handle it, that risk is minimal. Risk is further minimized by having the classroom teacher in total control of the actions of the discipline squad. The situation might go something like this:

1. A problem arises that is beyond the teacher's ability to manage safely.

2. The teacher calls loudly to the class, "Call the discipline squad!" Students have been told in advance what to do. Following those directions, some would immediately, say, phone the office, notify all nearby teachers, or run to the counselor's office.

3. Sometimes the call alone deflates the problem enough so that the teacher can handle it. However, the discipline squad will soon arrive. As members arrive, they stand and wait for commands from the classroom teacher. They do not initiate any actions without directions. The classroom teacher must be clearly in charge. If the problem has by then eased enough so that the teacher can handle it, the other adults can be thanked and dismissed. If not, the classroom teacher directs members of the squad, saying, for example, "Separate those two young men. Remind all others to take their seats. Take the one with the red shirt to the hall. Help me check the room for weapons. I'll start here. Mr. Jenkins, please begin there."

ASK FOR IDEAS

The purpose of asking for ideas is to broaden a teacher's base of options and supports. The strategy entails sharing problems with other professionals and requesting sugges-

tions. It is appropriate whenever additional ideas or a new perspective might be helpful.

A tradition has grown in schools that discourages teachers from asking for help with discipline problems. That is understandable. Many teachers, not knowing how to handle their problems, have sent so many students to others that it becomes easy to conclude that they themselves have not taken their management responsibilities seriously. It then seems logical to press all teachers to handle all their own classroom problems.

Teachers nowadays will do better with more support and practical assistance and *less* pressure. This is especially true in the case of serious discipline problems. Even experienced psychologists have difficulty knowing what to do with some of the students in schools today. It is unfair to expect teachers to know better.

I recommend that teachers ask for help early, not to avoid management responsibilities but to fulfill them more wisely, more humanely. I would include in any discipline plan the names of two or three people, other teachers perhaps, but not necessarily teachers, whom I knew I could approach any time I needed new ideas or an additional viewpoint. The more consultation, and the sooner, the more likely a wise and effective approach will be fashioned, to the benefit of students' welfare and teachers' dignity alike.

Glossary of Strategies

Note: The acronym *WW* following a term indicates that it is one of ten strategies adapted from *The Workshop Way®*, courtesy of Grace H. Pilon (1988).

Apologizing *Purpose*: To model a behavior important to the development of mature relationships. Also used to reduce guilt in the classroom. *Strategy*: The teacher offers a brief apology and perhaps discusses the advantages of students also using apologies. *When used*: As appropriate, following acts the teacher regrets having done.

Ask for ideas *Purpose*: To broaden the base of a teacher's options and supports. *Strategy*: The teacher shares problems with other professionals and requests suggestions. *When used*: Whenever additional ideas or a new perspective might be helpful.

"Be" choice *Purpose*: To teach students how they can bring out their best qualities. Also to help teachers bring into the classroom the personal qualities they most want to express. *Strategy*: The teacher shows students how to choose the way they want to be (be persistent, be courageous, be accepting, etc.). Teachers themselves use "be" choices (to be confident that students will cooperate; to be strong, warm, and well-organized, etc.). *When used*: Anytime appropriate.

Broken record *Purpose*: To enable the teacher to persist in asserting authority without arguing with students. *Strategy*: The teacher simply repeats a statement that a student seems not to be respecting. *When used*: When a student is unaware that he or she is not hearing the teacher's message. *(WW)*

Calamity procedure *Purpose*: To enable a teacher to regain control of a classroom that has slipped into chaos. *Strategy*: The teacher rapidly, forcefully calls out questions and directs students to write down the answers. *When used*: Whenever a class has gotten out of hand. *(WW)*

Calm reminder *Purpose*: To remind students what they are supposed to do. *Strategy*: Without communicating negative emotions, the teacher reminds students what they are supposed to do. *When used*: When it is appropriate to assume that a student simply has forgotten what to do.

Check-yourself message *Purpose*: To remind students to manage themselves responsibly. *Strategy*: The teacher tells students to check what they have done, implying that when they do so they will see what corrections are necessary. *When used*: When students become careless.

Class agreements *Purpose*: To communicate teacher respect for students' thoughts and feelings and encourage a classroom atmosphere of cooperation. *Strategy*: The teacher outlines plans for the class and invites student agreement. The teacher can also invite student suggestions. *When used*: As appropriate, perhaps every day or *only* when starting new units.

Clock focus *Purpose*: To settle restless students down and increase their powers of concentration. *Strategy*: The teacher announces, "Clock focus." Students know they are to stand and watch the second hand of a clock make full circles, as many rotations as they choose, and then to sit and resume their individual work. *When used*: Whenever students need to settle down, particularly young students working at individual study tasks. *(WW)*

Community living lessons *Purpose*: To increase appreciation of what is involved in living as a cooperative classroom community. *Strategy*: The teacher offers examples that define healthful community living and inspires students to become such a community. *When used*: From time to time, especially when it appears that students could do better at living and working together.

Conflict-resolution lesson *Purpose*: To teach students how to solve problems in a nondestructive, mutually respectful way. *Strategy*: The teacher shows students how to talk honestly about a conflict and, if talk alone does not ease the conflict, how to brainstorm and write a list of possible next steps. *When used*: Whenever the situation seems appropriate for students to learn conflict-resolution skills.

Cool-quick-certain control *Purpose*: To ensure physical safety when one or more students become dangerously out of control. *Strategy*: The teacher takes control promptly and forcefully and as unemotionally as possible. *When used*: If one or more students becomes dangerously out of control.

Cushioning *Purpose*: To minimize learning fears and produce confident, active learners. *Strategy*: The teacher reinforces truths about learning with questions (e.g., "Is it OK if someone gives a wrong answer today? Why?") and reminders (e.g., "As you tackle the homework, remember that you don't have to understand it all tonight.") *When used*: Frequently, especially before students are asked to participate in lessons. *(WW)*

Diagnosing student motivations *Purpose*: To explore what might be motivating a student to continue misbehaving. *Strategy*: The teacher considers alternative reasons for a student's behavior and, when appropriate, makes a plan to lead the student toward more healthful patterns of conduct. *When used*: When students persist in misbehaving.

Discipline squad *Purpose*: To give teachers who feel physically vulnerable adequate feelings of security. *Strategy*: The teacher arranges for several other educators in the building to respond in times of emergency. *When used*: When teachers feel too threatened to work effectively.

Dramatic distraction *Purpose*: To keep problems from getting worse and allow time for the positive energies of students to come forth. *Strategy*: The teacher forcefully turns attention away from problem behavior toward something more positive, such as a safe venting of feelings, or toward something nonemotional, such as a math puzzle or riddle. *When used*: In situations too emotionally intense for prompt, rational resolution. *(WW)*

Getting along and working well together *Purpose*: To inspire students to think about what they can do to improve the way they live and work together and to keep them moving in that direction. *Strategy*: The teacher announces that "getting along and working well together" is to be an objective of the class. The teacher also works to keep that objective in view over the long term. *When used:* Whenever appropriate.

Hand-raising signal *Purpose:* To switch efficiently from small-group discussions to teacher talk. *Strategy*: The teacher raises one hand; students who see the raised hand then raise one of their own hands, and all students then see it's time to stop talking. *When used*: When the teacher wants students to stop talking among themselves.

Honest "I" statements *Purpose*: To communicate honestly with students without generating defensiveness or guilt and to model a valuable interpersonal skill. *Strategy*: The teacher talks honestly about personal needs and feelings, making "I" statements, avoiding comments about what "you" did or "you" said. The teacher can also teach students how to do the same. *When used*: Especially useful when upsetting feelings emerge.

Intelligence call-up *Purpose*: To remind students that they are intelligent and inspire them to think problems through independently. *Strategy*: The teacher keeps generating awareness of the native intelligence of students, reminding them of their ability to stop and think and make responsible choices. *When used*: Frequently throughout the school year. *(WW)*

Mastery of student procedures *Purpose*: To prevent misbehavior and confusion about classroom procedures. *Strategy*: The teacher spends enough time teaching classroom procedures so that students can easily follow them. *When used*: At the beginning of a course.

Next-time message *Purpose*: To correct students' behavior without creating feelings of discouragement. *Strategy*: The teacher tells students what to do next time, not focusing on what was done this time. *When used*: As appropriate.

"Once" principle *Purpose*: To free the teacher from the need to repeat directions, and to teach students to listen responsibly and catch up appropriately. *Strategy*: The teacher announces that from now on he or she will give directions only once; students missing the directions are to find an intelligent way to catch up. *When used*: As early in a course or school year as possible. *(WW)*

Parent aides *Purpose*: To strengthen the adult presence in a classroom and increase school-parent cooperation. *Strategy*: The teacher invites parents or other adults to visit often and perhaps act as teacher aides. *When used*: As appropriate.

Person-to-person dialogue *Purpose*: To advance mutual understanding between teacher and student. *Strategy*: Teacher and student have a private dialogue, with the teacher mainly using honest "I" statements. *When used*: Especially when a student does not appear to appreciate the teacher's perspective.

Positive parent schedule *Purpose*: To increase family support for students. *Strategy*: The teacher prepares a schedule that makes it easy to give positive messages to all parents. *When used*: Early in the school year.

Reality-acceptance monologue *Purpose*: To "maintain sanity" when a student's annoying behavior persists. *Strategy*: The teacher accepts the fact that not all bothersome behavior can be eliminated and, as necessary, reminds himself or herself of that reality. *When used*: Especially when nothing works to improve a student's behavior.

Redirect student energy *Purpose*: To end misbehavior without creating negative feelings. *Strategy*: Instead of focusing on the misbehavior, the teacher turns student attention to something else, preferably something worth attending to. *When used*: When direct confrontation is either unnecessary or imprudent.

Self-acceptance monologue *Purpose*: To preserve a teacher's peace of mind. *Strategy*: The teacher reminds himself or herself that one cannot expect to perform perfectly at all times. *When used*: After acting less effectively than one would have wished.

Self-management contract *Purpose*: To solve a discipline problem in a way that cultivates a student's sense of responsibility and creates a win-win situation; also to show students how interpersonal conflicts can be resolved peacefully. *Strategy*: Three steps are involved: (1) a person-to-person dialogue aiming for mutual student-teacher understanding, (2) brainstorming to produce a written list of possible steps to ease the problem, and (3) a review of the list so that mutual agreement might be reached on an action plan. *When used*: Whenever needed.

Silent response *Purpose*: To give students room to solve their own problems while the teacher avoids a hasty, inappropriate response. *Strategy*: The teacher reacts to an act of misbehavior by making a mental note only and considering later what, if any, action is appropriate. *When used*: When an act of misbehavior is not dangerous. *(WW)*

Simple authority statement *Purpose*: To employ authority with minimum distress and emotion, and to show students how a person can use authority respectfully and reasonably. *Strategy*: The teacher voices disapproval authoritatively, promptly, and as unemotionally as possible. *When used*: When misbehavior requires teacher intervention.

Temporary removal *Purpose*: To give a teacher respite from a problem situation. *Strategy*: The teacher instructs a student to leave the group. *When used*: When it appears that no other strategic choice will work.

Truth signs *Purpose*: To teach a class key truths about what constitutes an effective, healthy learning community and to provide guidelines to help the class become such a group. *Strategy*: The teacher explains key truths about effective learning, such as "It's OK to make mistakes; that's the way we learn." The teacher also posts these key truths on signboards to serve as guidelines. *When used*: Early in a course. *(WW)*

Undone-work response *Purpose*: To respond wisely when students fail to do required work. *Strategy*: The teacher avoids a blaming response and instead aims to make a response that encourages growth. *When used*: When a student has not completed work on time.

Visitor's chair *Purpose*: To position a student close to the teacher without communicating displeasure. *Strategy*: The teacher asks a student to sit in a chair close to where the teacher is sitting or standing called the "visitor's chair." Students know they can return to their own seats whenever they feel ready for responsible self-management. *When used*: When a young student needs proximity to the teacher and time to regain personal composure. *(WW)*

Waiting place *Purpose*: To provide a convenient place for a misbehaving student to wait before having a dialogue with the teacher. *Strategy*: The teacher announces the place where a student is asked to wait until the teacher has time for a private conversation. *When used*: With young students, early in a course.

Whole-class problem solving *Purpose*: To get maximum input for solutions to a problem and maximum commitment to chosen actions, and to model a mature problem-resolution strategy. *Strategy*: Two steps are involved: (1) The class brainstorms and produces a written list of possible solutions. (2) The list is reviewed so that an action plan can be developed that is acceptable to both teacher and students. *When used*: When a particular problem involves a large portion of the class.

Whole-self lesson *Purpose*: To help students learn to accept themselves, accept others, and be open to becoming the best that they can currently be. *Strategy*: The teacher explains that everyone has narrow and open selves, and that when narrow selves show up, as they do for everyone, it's wise to be accepting, for acceptance opens people to their open selves and allows people to be their whole selves. *When used*: Whenever appropriate.

Bibliography

Adkins, G. 1990. Educating the handicapped in the regular classroom. *Educational Digest* 56(1): 24-27.

Ames, C., and Ames, R., eds. 1985. *Research on motivation in education.* Vol. 1, *Student motivation.* Orlando, Fla.: Academic Press.

Augustine, D. K.; Gruber, K. D.; and Hanson, L. R. 1990. Cooperation works! *Educational Leadership* 47(4): 4-7.

Bandura, A. 1965. Behavior modification through modeling procedures. In L. Krasner and L. P. Ullman, eds., *Research in behavior modification,* 310-40. New York: Holt, Rinehart, and Winston.

Biehler, R. F., and Snowman, J. 1990. *Psychology applied to teaching.* 6th ed. Boston: Houghton Mifflin.

Brandt, R. 1989. A changed professional culture. *Educational Leadership* 46(8): 2.

Brendtro, L.; Brokenleg, M.; and Bockern, S. V. 1990. *Reclaiming youth at risk.* Bloomington, Ind.: National Educational Service.

Brody, N. 1983. *Human motivation: Commentary on goal-directed action.* New York: Academic Press.

Brown, D. 1971. *Changing student behavior: A new approach to discipline.* Dubuque, Iowa: W. C. Brown.

Cangelosi, J. S. 1990. *Designing tests for evaluating student achievement.* White Plains, N.Y.: Longman.

Canter, L., and Canter, M. 1976. *Assertive discipline: A take-charge approach for today's educator.* Seal Beach, Calif.: Lee Canter and Associates.

———. 1989. *Assertive discipline for secondary school educators: Inservice video package and leader's manual.* Santa Monica, Calif.: Lee Canter and Associates.

Charles, C. M. 1992. *Building classroom discipline: From models to practice.* 6th ed. White Plains, N.Y.: Longman.

Cooper, H. 1989. *Homework.* White Plains, N.Y.: Longman.

Curwin, R. L., and Mendler, A. N. 1988. *Discipline with dignity.* Alexandria, Va.: Association for Supervision and Curriculum Development.

Dewey, J. 1933. *How we think.* rev. ed. Boston: D.C. Heath.

Doyle, W. 1986. Classroom organization and management. In M. C. Wittrock, ed., *Handbook of research on teaching.* 3d ed., 392-431. New York: Macmillan.

Dreikurs, R. 1968. *Psychology in the classroom.* 2d ed. New York: Harper and Row.

Dreikurs, R.; Grunwald, B.; and Pepper, F. 1982. *Maintaining sanity in the classroom.* 2d ed. New York: Harper and Row.

Englander-Golden, P., and Sater, V. 1990. *Say it straight.* Palo Alto, Calif.: Science and Behavior Books.

Firth, G. 1985. *Behavior management in the schools: A primer for parents.* New York: Thomas.

Gathercoal, F. 1990. *Judicious discipline.* 2d ed. San Francisco: Caddo Gap.

Ginott, H. G. 1972. *Teacher and child.* New York: Avon.

Glasser, W. 1985. *Control theory in the classroom.* New York: Perennial.

———. 1990. *The quality school: Managing students without coercion.* New York: Harper and Row.

Gordon, T. 1974. *Teacher effectiveness training.* New York: Dave McKay.

———. 1989. *Teaching children self-discipline: At home and at school.* New York: Times Books.

Harmin, M. 1990. The Workshop Way to student success. *Educational Leadership* 48(1): 43-47.

———. 1995. *Strategies to Inspire Active Learning.* Edwardsville, Ill.: Inspiring Strategy Institute.

Harris, T. A. 1969. *I'm OK, you're OK: A practical guide to transactional analysis.* New York: Harper and Row.

Hunkins, F. P. 1989. *Teaching thinking through effective questioning.* Boston: Christopher-Gordon.

Jones, F. 1987a. *Positive classroom discipline.* New York: McGraw-Hill.

———. 1987b. *Positive classroom instruction.* New York: McGraw-Hill.

Jones, V. F., and Jones, L. S. 1990. *Comprehensive classroom management: Motivating and managing students.* 3d ed. Boston: Allyn and Bacon.

Karlin, M. S., and Berger, R. 1972. *Discipline and the disruptive child: A practical guide for elementary teachers.* West Nyack, N.Y.: Parker.

Kerr, M. M., and Nelson, C. M. 1983. *Strategies for managing behavior problems in the classroom.* Columbus, Ohio: Merrill.

Knight, M. E. 1992. *Teaching children to love themselves: A handbook for parents and teachers of young children*. Hillside, N.J.: Vision.

Kobrin, D. 1992. *In there with kids: Teaching in today's classrooms*. Boston: Houghton Mifflin.

Kohut, S., and Range, D. G. 1979. *Classroom discipline: Case studies and viewpoints*. Washington, D.C.: National Education Association.

Kounin, J. 1977. *Discipline and group management in classrooms*. New York: Holt, Rinehart, and Winston.

Krumboltz, J. D., and Krumboltz, H. B. 1972. *Changing children's behavior*. Englewood Cliffs, N.J.: Prentice-Hall.

Lasley, T. J. 1985. Fostering nonaggression in the classroom: An anthropological perspective. *Theory into Practice* 24: 247-55.

Lemlich, J. 1988. *Classroom management: Methods and techniques for elementary and secondary teachers*. 2d ed. White Plains, N.Y.: Longman.

Martin, G., and Pear, J. 1983. *Behavior modification: What it is and how to do it*. 2d ed. Englewood Cliffs, N.J.: Prentice-Hall.

Maslow, A. 1962. *Toward a psychology of being*. New York: Van Nostrand.

Maurer, R. 1988. *Special educator's discipline handbook*. West Nyack, N.Y.: Center for Applied Research in Education.

McCarty, H. 1991. *The bottom line in school success*. Galt, Calif.: Hanoch McCarty and Associates.

McEwan, B. 1991. *Practicing judicious discipline: An educator's guide to a democratic classroom*. San Francisco: Caddo Gap.

McIntyre, T. 1989. *The behavior management handbook: Setting up effective behavior management systems*. Boston: Allyn and Bacon.

Moorman, C. 1985. *Talk Sense to Yourself*. Portage, Mich.: Personal Power Press.

Ornstein, A. C. 1990. *Strategies for effective teaching*. New York: Harper and Row.

Pilon, G. H. 1988. *The Workshop Way*. New Orleans, La.: Workshop Way.

Pulaski, M. A. S. 1980. *Understanding Piaget: An introduction to children's cognitive development*. 2d ed. New York: Harper and Row.

Purkey, W. W., and Novak, J. M. 1984. *Inviting school success: A self-concepts approach to teaching and learning*. 2d ed. Belmont, Calif.: Wadsworth.

Pysch, R. 1991. Discipline improves as students take responsibility. *NASSP Bulletin* 75: 117-18.

Redl, F., and Wattenberg, W. 1951, 1959. *Mental hygiene in teaching*. New York: Harcourt, Brace, and World.

Reider, B. 1988. *A hooray kind of kid: A child's self-esteem and how to build it*. El Dorado Hills, Calif.: Sierra House.

Render, G.; Padilla, J.; and Krank, H. 1989. What research really shows about assertive discipline. *Educational Leadership* 46(6): 72-75.

Rogoff, B. 1990. *Apprenticeship in thinking*. New York: Oxford University Press.

Rosenthal, R., and Jacobson, L. 1968. *Pygmalion in the classroom: Teacher expectations and pupils' intellectual development*. New York: Holt, Rinehart, and Winston.

Sizer, T. R. 1992. *Horace's school: Redesigning the American high school*. Boston: Houghton Mifflin.

Skinner, B. F. 1953. *Science and human behavior*. New York: Macmillan.

———. 1971. *Beyond freedom and dignity*. New York: Knopf.

Slavin, R. E. 1991. Synthesis of research on cooperative learning. *Educational Leadership* 48(5): 71-82.

Swartz, R. J., and Perkins, D. N. 1990. *Teaching thinking: Issues and approaches*. rev. ed. Pacific Grove, Calif.: Midwest.

Swick, K. J. 1985. *Disruptive student behavior in the classroom*. 2d ed. Washington, D.C.: National Education Association.

Tillman, M. 1982. *Trouble-shooting classroom problems*. Glenview, Ill.: Scott, Foresman.

Van Dyke, H. T. 1984. Corporal punishment in our schools. *The Clearing House* 57: 296-300.

Walker, H., and Sylwater, R. 1991. Where is school along the path to prison? *Educational Leadership* 49(1): 14-16.

Walker, H. M. 1979. *The acting-out child: Coping with classroom disruptions*. Boston: Allyn and Bacon.

Walker, J. E., and Shea, T. M. 1984. *Behavior management: A practical approach for educators*. 3d ed. St. Louis, Mo.: Times Mirror/Mosby College.

Wilde, J., and Sommers, P. 1978. Teaching disruptive adolescents: A game worth winning. *Phi Delta Kappan* 59: 342-43.

Wynne, E. A., and Ryan, K. 1991. *Reclaiming our schools: A handbook on teaching character, academics, and discipline*. New York: Macmillan.